# LAKERS
# KOMAIYA

## 50
### LESSONS *to* PRIME YOUR
### BEST SELF

# DEVELOPING
# THE
# GREATNESS
# WITHIN YOU

## HOW ORDINARY PEOPLE TAKE THE LEAP
## *to* LEAD *a* LIFE *of* IMPACT

**TRIBE** OF **DAVID**

ISBN (paperback): 978-0-6483799-0-4
ISBN (audiobook): 978-0-6483799-2-8
ISBN (ebook): 978-0-6483799-3-5

**Printed in Australia**

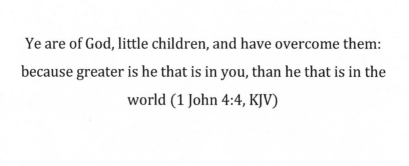

Ye are of God, little children, and have overcome them: because greater is he that is in you, than he that is in the world (1 John 4:4, KJV)

This book is dedicated to:

God - the one who has invested greatness in us all.

Morenikeji, my precious wife and best friend – you are indeed a treasure.

My sons, Timothy and Victor - you keep inspiring me to develop the greatness in me.

My parents, Pa Michael and Madam Fidelia – you sowed in me the core values that I continue to reap from.

My siblings – you have always believed in me.

All the people God has used to shape my life – upon your shoulders I stand today.

# CONTENTS

# Introduction

What is greatness? The dictionary defines it as "the quality of being great; eminence or distinction."

Everybody has a potential to be great. The question however is, "Are you willing to pay the price to develop your unique greatness?"

Whether you are a single mother, a teenager, a business executive, an employee, a spiritual overseer, we are all destined for greatness. Greater is He that is in you than he that is in the world.

The words and ideas that fill the pages that follow are not abstract concepts to me; they represent thoughts and practices that continue to challenge me as I develop my unique greatness.

For several years, I have keenly observed with great curiosity how passionate men and women continue to evolve into their best selves. I perceive that by devotion to some comprehensible practices, they have taken a leap to lead a life of impact. Consequently, some of the materials in this book are lessons I have gathered during my personal devotion and reflection. Others came about as a result of my dedication to researching what exactly move the needle for those individuals who have been able to unleash the unique greatness in their life.

Therefore, what you will find in this book are timeless lessons gleaned from great individuals in the Bible and also in our contemporary world.

My intention is that this book becomes a roadmap for you

as you develop your unique greatness. In the light of this, there are a couple of ways you can engage with this book. You can use it as a 50-day devotional, reading each lesson, praying, making your confession and renewing your mind in the process. You can also read and action each lesson chronologically or otherwise as it suits your exploration of the book. I want to encourage you, whichever way you choose to use it however, to discipline yourself to reflect and write down your action plan and execute. This is the most crucial aspect of the process of renewing your mind to developing your unique greatness.

This book might become quite personal to you as you make relevant notes and highlights (or dog-ears) which you may need to refer to again and again. Feel free to date your thoughts and put a time frame by which you want to have actioned your plans. As we can never graduate from the school of greatness, it is my hope that this book becomes a timeless resource.

Finally, this book indeed is a culmination of the wisdom learned in ten years in my personal journey and in helping and encouraging people to develop the greatness within them. Now I have the opportunity to share them with you.

A toast to your evolving greatness.

Lakers Komaiya

# THE BANE OF THE FAMILIAR

*Scripture Reading*
*God told Abram: "Leave your country, your family, and your father's home for a land that I will show you"* (Genesis 12:1).

*What is familiar is what we are used to; what we are used to is most difficult to "know."*

*– Friedrich Nietzsche*

The starting point of partnership [walking] with God is to move away from what is familiar. His ways and acts are different from yours. Walking with someone opens you up to the world of how they think, feel, act, and deal with the general and specific issues of life. Walking away from the familiar, the usual, and your comfort zone to achieve your dream is not an option, it is a requirement.

> The starting point of partnership with God is to move away from what is familiar.

The outcome you crave as a leader in your field will be realized when you obey and move in a direction consistent with God's instructions. To achieve this, you must separate your thinking and mindset from that of the crowd. Giving in to the familiar will prevent you from exploring, as well as reaping the unusual goodness and treasures that are waiting to be uncovered.

Certainly, those who are next in line for greatness do not permit fear or anxiety to rule their lives. They are driven by their commitment to the ultimate realization of the vision they have previewed. I want you to always remember that your actions are indications of what you truly believe. The more time you spend with God, the more you can trust your instincts to lead and guide you in the path of righteousness. You can believe that even with the unfamiliar, goodness and mercy will attend to you.

*Reflection*
Identify the familiar thoughts that are self-limiting and inhibiting the realization of your dream.

*Confession*
I am next in line for greatness. I do not permit anxiety to rule my life. I believe that even with the unfamiliar, goodness and mercy will attend to me.

*Write down the relevant practical steps you need to make the new insight a reality, and the time to implement it.*

| Practical steps | Time |
|---|---|
| | |

# THE START-USE-DO PRINCIPLE

*Scripture Reading*
*And I will make you a great nation, and I will bless you*
*[with abundant increase of favors] and make your name*
*famous and distinguished, and you will be a blessing*
*[dispensing good to others* (Genesis 12:2).*

*To achieve greatness, **start** where you are, **use** what you*
*have, **do** what you can.*

*– Arthur Ashe*

bram's motivation was kept alive even though he had no child as evidence that God's promise to him would be a reality. He had nothing to grasp physically, but he held on to the promise. You too can hold on to a visual or a mental image of the promise. In other words, focus

> *It is important to rely on God, for He has promised, "I will make you..."*

on the God-given picture of the dream, grow expectancy, and proactively work and partner with Him every day. I have noticed that in our attempts to achieve dreams or visions, most of us labor in our own strength. Worst still, we look to some individual to "make" us. However, it is important for us to rely on God alone, for He has promised, "I will make you..." A wise man once said, "If someone can make you, then they can break you." The God who has impregnated you with a seed that has the capacity to become a forest is also the One who can make you great beyond your wildest imagination.

Understandably, when we think of the magnitude of the vision God has given us the privilege to see, the resources needed to accomplish the task overwhelm us. Be encouraged today. Don't be paralyzed by what you don't have. Keep working with what you have. You are the one chosen to bring about the vision you have been pleasured to imagine.

Therefore, start where you are; use what you have and do what you can. This is not the time to pass the buck. The vision has been given to you. Own it. Feel it. Act it. Shake off doubt or low self-esteem. Blessed with a God-idea, you have to be committed and willing to play your part to bring about its realization. Don't push the fulfilment of your dream to someone else. Go live it. It's your destiny!

*Reflection*
God said to an individual, Abram, "I will make you a great nation." How are you responding to the seeming "impossible" promise He has given you?

What do you need to do to agree with God and realize the vision He has given to you?

*Confession*
I walk in line with God's promise for me today. I can do all things through Christ who gives me strength.

*Write down the relevant practical steps you need to make the new insight a reality, and the time to implement it.*

| Practical steps | Time |
|---|---|
| | |

# MIND STRETCH

### Scripture Reading

*So Abraham departed, as the Lord had directed him; and Lot [his nephew] went with him. Abram was seventy-five years old when he left Haran* (Genesis 12:4).

*The mind, once stretched by a new idea, never returns to its original dimensions.*

*– Ralph Waldo Emerson*

God wants to establish His prominence here on earth as it is in heaven. So He is always looking for people to "possess the land." This traverses the business, political, technological, social, entertainment, family, and spiritual spheres. He wants to fill the earth with His glory by empowering you to be fruitful, to multiply, subdue, and dominate it (Genesis 1:28). Hence, you can be assured that His idea and direction will always stretch you.

But wait! How do you treat the ideas and intentions that show up on the screen of your mind? Stretching your mind denotes you will have to vacate your status quo. It means you have to be willing to step into the unknown. Your imagination is one of the ways you receive divine instructions from God. Do not be afraid when you begin to get mind-blowing insights. Moreover, do not allow your current resources to limit you from walking consistently with the instruction you receive. When God chooses to collaborate with you, He will call you up to His level, not the other way around. Let Him open your mind and spirit to the vast capital that is available to you. Take time to quieten your mind daily so He can impart knowledge to you. Great people seem to be used to this mode of instruction. They do not second-guess themselves. They understand that the mandate typically becomes clearer as they obey and act on God's direction. You have been chosen to represent a heavenly organization here on earth. Obedience is mainly for your advantage. Therefore, allow a God-idea (or God-think) to stretch your mind today. However, don't stop there. Turn the insights into actions and results.

> *Do not be afraid when you begin to get mind-blowing insights.*

*Reflection*

Are you running with the idea God has birthed in you or are you still second-guessing yourself?

*Confession*

I have a mandate to carry out in my area of influence, for I have been chosen to represent the heavenly organization here on earth.

*Write down the relevant practical steps you need to make the new insight a reality, and the time to implement it.*

| Practical steps | Time |
| --- | --- |
|  |  |

# FOLLOW INSIGHT WITH ACTION

*Scripture Reading*
*Arise; walk through the land, the length of it and the breadth of it, for I will give it to you* (Genesis 13:17).

*The key to success is action, and the essential in action is perseverance.*

*– Sun Yat-sen*

God always accompanies new insights with a call to action. Faith without works is dead (James 2:17). In other words, when you visualize your dream, you begin to create a mental image of possibility. Have you been sitting in the same spot for a long time? Have you blamed everyone and everything imaginable for your status quo? The only place such attitudes will get you is "nowhere." However, if you review that limiting mindset today and arise, things will start to change for you. I challenge you. Take the first step and begin to walk towards your destiny.

"Walking" enables you to see what God sees. That is to say, you recognize what others are oblivious to. In the process, your sense of perception becomes well-developed. You see opportunities where others see failure and surplus where others see lack. Mark 11:23 says, "You will have what you say." You not only have what you profess, you also have what you see. What you "see" is what you get. If you see nothing, you get nothing. Where untrained eyes see a vacant plot of land, an empty space or worse still "nothing," estate developers see apartments, buildings, businesses, investment opportunities, shopping malls etc.

> God always accompanies new insights with a call to action.

There is a popular story about two salesmen dispatched from the headquarters of a product-manufacturing factory to a remote part of the world. After the initial survey on arrival, the first salesman sent back an email advising his manager, "The market here is discouraging. No one uses our product in this place. I'll be catching the next plane out in a day or two." In contrast, his colleague sent an email that read, "Wow, this is exciting! No one has heard about our product in this place. The people are open to exploring new merchandise. Please send more shipments of our products. The potential for market dominance here is huge." Walking through the "length and breadth" of what you intend to possess may be hard work. However, God is interested in reconnaissance. You need to be equipped with valuable knowledge of what you are going to possess; understand the terrain; know the language; recognize the landscape; become familiar with the risks that may be involved and plan ahead to mitigate them. Even though you need to plan ahead, act from your current position. Walk and keep walking until you realize your dreams.

*When you visualize your dream, you begin to create a mental image of possibility.*

*Reflection*

What information should you acquire to take the next step towards the realization of your dream? Act now!

*Confession*

The whole earth is waiting for the manifestation of my dream. My journey has begun. I am walking towards the realization of my dreams.

*Write down the relevant practical steps you need to make the new insight a reality, and the time to implement it.*

| Practical steps | Time |
|---|---|
| | |

LESSON 5

# NEVER SLAM THE DOOR

*Scripture Reading*
*And there was strife between the herdsmen of Abram's cattle and the herdsmen of Lot's cattle. And the Canaanite and the Perizzite were dwelling then in the land [making fodder more difficult to obtain]* (Genesis 13:14).

*Peace is not absence of conflict; it is the ability to handle conflict by peaceful means.*
*– Ronald Regan*

How do you treat people who see things differently from you? Do you slam the door in their faces? As you work with your team to achieve goals and objectives, occasions of disagreement will arise. I have noticed that differences in opinion may occur as a result of conflicting facts, views, interests or claims. In

> *People who want to be influential protect relationships.*

fact, it is typical for people to have contradictory views even while assessing the same situation. This was the case at the dress rehearsal of an event I hosted monthly called "The Tribe of David." The stage was finally set after a grueling two hours workout. Suddenly, I noticed that what I had perceived as an excellent floral arrangement by one of our sponsors had been changed. While I appreciated the adjustment, I kindly requested that the previous floral display be restored. The moral of this is that in the event of a clash of ideas, you should demonstrate you respect the right of the other party to have her/his opinion just as you have a right to yours.

As you develop the greatness within you, you will begin to recognize that one of the outstanding qualities of smart leaders is their crisis management and conflict resolution expertise. This suggests that you need to be comfortable to dwell, communicate, and reason with people who may not share the same ideologies as you. Your intention is to win them, not offend them.

By now, people loyal to Abram and Lot were at loggerheads over resource sharing. Abram, however, recognized he had to be careful not to destroy what he had labored to build. He would not jeopardize his relationship and investment in his nephew, Lot. A wise man once said, "The measure of a durable relationship lies in conflict management." People who want to be influential protect relationships. Often, they are willing to sacrifice material things to preserve important aspects of their affiliations. Self-centredness would have caused Abram to act differently. Even as a mentor, he chose not to burn bridges. Yes, if necessary, separate but maintain a passage for continued contact, especially as a mentee. You'll need it!

Finally, be firm, yet, gentle as you attempt to manage conflict today. Regardless of your position, never slam the door in the face of someone who may share a different opinion. Access to the complementary viewpoint you resist now might be beneficial to you in the future.

## Reflection

How better can you manage situations that typically result in conflict in your relationships, career, and life in general?

## Confession

I am blessed to be a blessing. I recognize the different standpoints those around me may have, but I still position myself to be a blessing to them.

*Write down the relevant practical steps you need to make the new insight a reality, and the time to implement it.*

| Practical steps | Time |
| --- | --- |
|  |  |

# DEVIATING FROM THE NORM

*Scripture Reading*
*And they said, "Come, let us build us a city and a tower whose top reaches into the sky, and let us make a name for ourselves, lest we are scattered over the whole earth"* (Genesis 11:4).

*You never change things by fighting the existing reality. To change something, build a new model that makes the existing model obsolete.*

*– Buckminster Fuller*

Most times, we continue to engage in the same activity and expect a different outcome. However, wisdom requires you to know when to change tack. These men reported in Genesis 11 possessed the expertise to gather raw materials, bake bricks, conceptualize and draw the plan for the city, and engineer the structure.

> *Wisdom requires you to know when to change tack.*

They were willing to deviate from the norm. This means they risked building vertically, rather than horizontally, which was unusual in their days. The vision of the outcome was clear even though it was the first of its kind.

Seven things to consider as you contemplate deviating from the norm:

## 1. Believe something few others believe

You don't have to know something no one else knows; you simply need to raise the bar on your belief. Self-doubt and double-mindedness have a chance of terminating your dreams even before the pessimists do. Remember, most people do not see what you have been privileged to perceive. Therefore, be careful not to rely on their feedback. On occasions, it may not be constructive.

## 2. Be willing to ignore the usual

A concept in psychology called "Habituation" is defined as a decrease in response to a stimulus after repeated presentations. For example, a fragrance from a new perfume may initially draw your attention or be off-putting. Nevertheless, over time, as you become familiar with this smell, you pay less attention to the stimulus and your response to the fragrance diminishes.

It is typical to habituate to what is usual. Look out for what may be exceptional in things you would normally be oblivious to. Occasionally, set aside a moment and allow your mind to overlook the normal.

## 3. Be ready to abandon the status quo

Most people want things to change in their lives, but they don't want to change. They forget that they are the "change" they so much crave for. Denzel Washington once remarked, "Ease is a greater threat to progress than hardship." Someone said, "It is only human to approach pleasure and avoid pain." However, your current comfort can also become the enemy of your advancement in life. Remember, no pain, no gain. Therefore, you may need to reconsider this: "What pain do I need to endure in the service of doing things differently?"

## 4. Seek out appropriate tools/leverage

Abraham Lincoln once said, "Give me six hours to chop down a tree and I will spend the first four sharpening the axe." This statement underscores the importance of using appropriately tried and tested tools for the activities you have decided to tackle. Use of the wrong tools may exacerbate frustration and disappointment. Consider networking and partnering with people who can spur you on to be the best version of yourself.

## 5. Challenge yourself to engage in a new activity. Do something you have always been afraid of doing.

The problem that infuriates you the most is the one you have been assigned to solve. Everything in life is a solution to a problem — you included! You have been designed to be a solution to or bring a solution to a particular problem. You simply need to develop your passion, stay committed, and persevere against the odds.

## 6. Stretch your thinking and perception

Challenge your mind. Look at things from a different perspective. When trying to get people to see things differently, I often invite them to look at the situation "wearing the shoes" of the other person in question. Depending on their locations, two people can have different perspectives on the same object in a room. Allow your mind to come to terms with the fact that your current frame of reference is one of the so many possibilities that exist. Fifty years ago, who would have thought that most children in the world today would have computers they can carry folded and popped in a bag or even in their pockets?

## 7. Live courageously

Don't let fear stop you from trying. The only person who has not failed in life is the one who has not tried. Understand that failure is not the opposite of success; it is part of the process of winning. Nelson Mandela remarked, "Courage is not the absence of fear, but the triumph over it. The brave man is not he who does not feel afraid, but he who conquers that fear." You don't need to fight, avoid or deny the dread. It is acceptable to acknowledge your fear. But more importantly, it is also okay to do it *[fill in the gap with what you are anxious about]* afraid!

*Reflection*

What would you do if you knew failure is simply overrated?

*Confession*

Feel free to make up and write down your confession.

*Write down the relevant practical steps you need to make the new insight a reality, and the time to implement it.*

| Practical steps | Time |
| --- | --- |
|  |  |

# SEEK COLLABORATION

*Scripture Reading*
*But Lot, who went with Abram, also had flocks and herds and tents* (Genesis 13:5).

*Alone we can do so little; together we can do so much.*
*– Helen Keller*

A wise man once said, "If you want to go fast, go alone. If you want to go far, go together." I've discovered that, indeed, there is a time to go alone and there is a time to seek collaboration. When you are first starting out in any endeavor, you need to cast a clear vision, set the pace, and demonstrate personal commitment to show the world the value of your offering. Though you are aware you need the support of a dream team to bring your vision to completion, never be afraid to initiate your mission alone. As you make personal progress, you will realize when it is time to seek collaboration or build a supporting cast.

I love the way Helen Keller puts it. Alone, you can really go fast; however, you will achieve little in comparison with working with others. Consider running a 100-meter dash as going alone and a 4 X 100-meter relay race as working with a team. The relay team covers four times the distance covered by the individual sprinter. Going alone versus collaborating may spell the difference between being a "flash in the pan" and making a lasting impact. Collaboration allows you to leverage the skills, talents, and perspectives of others in your circle.

> If you want to go fast, go alone. If you want to go far, go together.

Seeking collaboration requires the development of excellent relational skills. The day I realized that human beings, in general, want to win in life, I changed my approach to relating to people. I worked it out that if I can help them win in an area that is meaningful to them, they will do everything to help me succeed too. In other words, make your interaction with people a win-win situation. Don't be self-centered or self-absorbed with simply achieving your objectives. Ensure you seek partnership with people who share similar values and principles with you.

Another aspect of forming a positive alliance is to seek mentorship. Mentoring fast tracks your progress and puts you in a vantage position. In addition, you have access to the wisdom and knowledge of those who have gone ahead of you, and you have the opportunity to build on their successes too.

**3 things to remember as you seek collaboration:**

1. Don't attempt to go it all alone lest you fall into the trap of "re-inventing the wheel."
2. Don't be an inconvenience to people who have been of help to you. Rather, ensure you bring benefits to them.
3. Don't be insensitive or cold to their needs. In other words, don't turn a blind eye to their requests. Let them know they can count on you. Have their backs.

*Reflection*

What meaningful associations do you require to take your vision to the next level?

*Confession*

I am sensitive to the needs of others. I recognize the meaningful associations necessary to take my vision to the next level.

*Write down the relevant practical steps you need to make the new insight a reality, and the time to implement it.*

| Practical steps | Time |
| --- | --- |
|  |  |

# STARVE CONFLICT OF OXYGEN

*Scripture Reading*

*And there was strife between the herdsmen of Abram's cattle and the herdsmen of Lot's cattle. And the Canaanite and the Perizzite were dwelling then in the land [making fodder more difficult to obtain]* (Genesis 13:7).

*Conflict cannot survive without your participation.*
*– Wayne Dyer*

Having access to other people's resources by collaborating with them will also leave you exposed to the occasional conflict of interest or differences in opinion. Be mindful of people who may want to start a skirmish that may tarnish what you have invested yourself in and spent a reasonable time building. They may be people who are not operating at the same wavelength as you. Beware! They might seek to cause drama in your life that may undermine your effectiveness.

Why do conflicts arise?

1. **People pitting you against other individuals or organizations.**

   Conflict may be triggered when others measure you against people in your or other fields. If left unchecked, this may lead to unhealthy competition or rivalry.

2. **People's attitudes towards the availability of or accessibility to resources and capital.**

   Whether you have abundance or scarcity, your mentality will go a long way in determining how you relate to others and how you are related to. This is especially true in the area of your achievement of personal and business objectives.

3. **People perceiving that there is a threat to their needs, objectives, goals or concerns.**

   Notice I used the word "perception." The threat does not need to be real to engender conflict. The way the situation is conceived or understood by either party may still bring about conflict.

   > *Do your best to strive for a win-win solution every time, all the time.*

   Ensure you inculcate a surplus mindset in the people around you. Equip them with conflict resolution skills. Do your best to collaborate, rather than compete. Strive for a win-win solution every time, all the time. In every win-lose relationship, be it business or personal, the "loser" eventually backs out of the relationship. This means the "winner" loses in the long run. Be the great person who is willing to lift others up. Let others experience the better deal they have relating to or doing business with you.

*Reflection*
What conflict have you experienced recently?
How could it have been handled differently for a better outcome?

*Confession*
I receive the wisdom to relate well and lift others up, especially people in my area of influence.

*Write down the relevant practical steps you need to make the new insight a reality, and the time to implement it.*

| Practical steps | Time |
|---|---|
|  |  |
|  |  |
|  |  |

# EXPAND YOUR FISH TANK

*Scripture Reading*
*Now the land was not able to nourish and support them so they could dwell together, for their possessions were too great for them to live together* (Genesis 13:6).

*The term "natural resources" confuses people. "Natural resources" are not like a finite number of gifts under a Christmas tree. Nature is given, but resources are created.*

*– Alex Tabarrok*

E very relationship will be tested. Most times, one sure test influencers face is how they respond to conflict when it arises. This is even more critical when the conflict involves people they have been a blessing to or continue to bless. At this time, potential great leaders may feel like they have been backstabbed.

The following are signs to look for that suggest you are beginning to resent someone you have been a blessing to in the past:

1. Feeling your beneficiary is suddenly ungrateful of past support and benefits received from you.
2. Reflecting on and rehashing the sacrifices you made in the past to make your beneficiary comfortable.
3. Feeling "taken for a ride," insulted, exploited or taken advantage of.
4. Feeling being a blessing to the beneficiary is now a curse to you.
5. Perceiving every progressive step the beneficiary takes now makes you stagnant on your journey.

One of the common reasons for conflict is competition over access to resources, potential clients or customers, markets etc. How do you handle someone who you may have helped in the past — to start a business, to identify or release their potential, or used your platform to promote — who you

> *Prosperity will always spawn new sets of challenges.*

now perceive to be a competitor? Understand that there are other individuals who may be interested in the same things you are. These are people you may be on the same greatness path as.

Consider reflecting on the following to reduce the instances of conflict:

1. Be mindful of factors that sustain growth and nourishment.
2. Replenish the source to support continued growth and prosperity.

3. Explore expansion of your sources and resources to support sustained nourishment.
4. Enter an empowering discussion and collaboration, rather than compete as you locate emerging markets.

Prosperity will always spawn new sets of challenges. Be ready to address them. Don't wait until you "feel" antagonized.

*Reflection*
What limiting thoughts or beliefs do I have about expanding my sources and resources?

How can I explore or create new sources and resources?

*Confession*
Feel free to make up and write down your confession.

*Write down the relevant practical steps you need to make the new insight a reality, and the time to implement it.*

| Practical steps | Time |
|---|---|
|  |  |

# WHO'S ON YOUR CREDIT LIST?

*Scripture Reading*

*When Samuel rose early to meet Saul in the morning, he was told, Saul came to Carmel, and behold, he set up for himself a monument or trophy [of his victory] and passed on and went down to Gilgal (1 Samuel 15:12).*

*It is amazing what you can accomplish if you do not care who gets the credit.*

*– Harry S. Truman*

B e careful how you choose to celebrate your accomplishments. It is easy to claim you have worked so hard to get to where you are today. You want to convince yourself that "I have paid my dues; hence, I deserve to win and be applauded." You may

> Do you think about others who may have helped you win?

even have a sense of entitlement, believing that the world owes you something it has just paid. But have you paused to think about the following?

1. Do you think about others who may have helped you get your win?
2. Have you considered openly recognizing them?
3. Do you recognize the sacrifices others have made to ensure your win?
4. Have you acknowledged God?
5. Does your win celebrate the cause or the individual, that is, you?

When you make wins about yourself and not about the team or the cause, like Saul in our scripture reading, you simply "pass on and go down." In other words, you pass on or throw away the credibility and respect people initially had for you. Since you have chosen to celebrate the achievement alone, you deny the compounding effect that could have been if you conceded to others who made the win possible. In the long run, you go down because you have failed to acknowledge the team that facilitated your success.

If you have ever fallen prey to an insensitive attitude like this, please consider reviewing your approach. Even those who engage in individual sports like boxing, powerlifting, skiing, and cycling are known to have a team of people behind them working tirelessly to bring out the best in them. Mia Hamm, a retired American professional soccer player, two-time Olympic gold medallist, and two-time FIFA Women's World Cup Champion, succinctly remarked, "I am a member of a team, and I rely on the team. I defer to it and sacrifice for it because the team, not the individual, is the ultimate champion." If you want a lasting win, understand that achievement is only sustained by a collective effort.

*Reflection*
Who have you failed to acknowledge in your past wins?

How can you make it up to them?

*Confession*
Feel free to make up and write down your confession.

*Write down the relevant practical steps you need to make the new insight a reality, and the time to implement it.*

| Practical steps | Time |
| --- | --- |
|  |  |
|  |  |
|  |  |
|  |  |

# WHY DO YOU DO WHAT YOU DO?

*Scripture Reading*

*I regret making Saul king, for he has turned back from following Me and has not performed My commands. And Samuel was grieved and angry [with Saul], and he cried to the Lord all night* (1 Samuel 15:11).

*We would frequently be ashamed of our good deeds if people saw all of the motives that produced them.*

*– Francois De La Rochefoucauld*

Saul, as a leader, seemed to have forgotten that God was the one who made him a king over Israel. Saul started listening to the people. Hence, he felt a need to carry out their requests rather than

> *If your motive was projected on a screen for all to see, will you still be able to stand tall?*

obey God. Before you became a success in your career, relationship, or ministry, you paid premium attention to listening and receiving guidance from God. However, you may have noticed lately that you are now more concerned with opinion polls, being politically correct than being righteous or that your guidance system has shifted from internal to external. If so, it's time for a motive check.

Consider the following:

1. Why do you do what you do?
2. What is your motive?
3. If your motive was projected on a screen for all to see, will you still be able to stand tall or will you cringe under a rock?
4. Is your motive God-honoring?

If Samuel were oblivious to God's initial command to Saul, Saul would have fooled him into believing that he was truly interested in worshipping the Lord with the best of the sheep and oxen taken from the Amalekites. People may temporarily succeed in hiding their real motives or intentions in the service of a good cause. Saul earnestly carried out God's command at first. However, as time passed, and he became cocky with fame and power, he sought to remain popular with the people.

What's your leadership style? Do you simply throw out a questionnaire or polls to determine what the people want and give it to them? Or are you convinced of what the vision or strategy is, communicate it clearly, and run with it? If you perceive that men made you who you are today, then you are bound to follow their commands. It is said, "He who pays the piper dictates the tunes." That may be true. However, it's better to remain connected to the One who predestined you. Rest assured, God leads and guides, as a mentor would do.

There is an unseen Force that can make a mere individual rise to the position of kingship. He will create a demand or a need that only the individual can meet. The Bible is silent about whether Saul was an ardent follower of God before he was made a king. While Saul was a product of the people's choice, David was clearly God's pick for the Jewish nation. Be careful not to delegate or put people who may not follow or share your principles or values in positions of authority. In time, they may choose to serve their own purposes rather than the cause for which they were chosen.

*Reflection*
Is the reason (overt) you provide to people consistent with the "real" reason (covert) why you do what you do?

*Confession*
Feel free to make up and write down your confession.

*Write down the relevant practical steps you need to make the new insight a reality, and the time to implement it.*

| Practical steps | Time |
| --- | --- |
|  |  |

# ARE YOU COURTING THE ENEMY?

*Scripture Reading*

*I regret making Saul king, for he has turned back from following Me and has not performed My commands. And Samuel was grieved and angry [with Saul], and he cried to the Lord all night* (1 Samuel 15:11).

*Much can be inferred about a man from his mistress: in her one beholds his weaknesses and his dreams.*

*– Georg C. Lichtenberg*

Now Saul, who had been reigning over the nation of Israel as a king for a while, had fought and won some battles. In his latest campaign, he was instructed to fight and destroy an old enemy. This adversary set himself earlier against Israel when they were coming out of servitude in Egypt. Saul complied with the instruction but half-heartedly. In other words, contrary to the directive, he saved and kept part of what he was meant to have destroyed for himself. Like Saul, some of us

> Sleeping with a scorpion under your duvet may later prove fatal.

struggle with issues from our past, which should have been done away with. These may include destructive habits, toxic relationships, secret lusts, and worldly pleasures. Occasionally, we succumb to being lured into the past to enjoy these "pleasures." In this state, we may continue to rationalize these actions to the point where we even justify our behaviors when confronted by our conscience or individuals to whom we are accountable. Like Saul, we fail to realize that sleeping with a scorpion under our duvet may later prove fatal.

Consider these questions as you ponder on past indulgences:

1. How do you relate to worldly pleasures in your heart?
2. Do you secretly wish you could enjoy what you consider you are missing?
3. Do you find a reason to indulge in what you know you should abstain from?
4. What are you meant to have conquered that you still have a close and intimate relationship with?
5. Do you sometimes find immoral things attractive?
6. Do you disguise evil in a good garb so you can enjoy it?
7. What do you secretly romance that may eventually compromise your integrity?
8. What alliance does your organization endorse that may eventually catalyze its disintegration?
9. Have you extinguished all destructive habits or are you still holding on to reminders?

10. Do you find pleasant and enjoyable what God considers abominable in His sight?
11. Are you offering "strange fires" unto God? Strange fires include profane practices and behaviors that contaminate your worship or service.

If you answered any of the above questions in the affirmative, you need to seriously ponder the sure consequences of your behavior if you fail to admit to your waywardness and repent.

*Reflection*
If God shines His light into the recesses of your heart, what will He find? It's time to repent.

*Confession*
Feel free to make up and write down your confession.

*Write down the relevant practical steps you need to make the new insight a reality, and the time to implement it.*

| Practical steps | Time |
| --- | --- |
| | |

# TAKE THE STONE AWAY

*Scripture Reading*
*Jesus said, "Take away the stone. Martha, the sister of the dead man, exclaimed, But Lord, by this time he [is decaying and] throws off an offensive odor, for he has been dead four days!"* (John 11:39).

*Every person takes the limit of their field of vision as the limits of the world.*

– Arthur Schopenhauer

New York Times Best Selling Author, John C. Maxwell, in most of his books on leadership commented on what he described as the "Law of the Lid." He remarked, "Leadership ability is the lid that determines a person's level of effectiveness. The lower an individual's ability to lead, the lower the lid on his potential. The higher the

> *Are you ready to lift the lid or roll the stone of ineffectiveness away?*

individual's ability to lead, the higher the lid on his potential."

Mary and Martha had just reached out to Jesus consequent to the death of their brother Lazarus. Jesus eventually showed up and was taken to the tomb where Lazarus had been laid. The first thing He did was to ask that the stone over the mouth of the tomb be taken away. His intention was to get the sisters, family members, and people of the city to understand they had a part to play in what was about to unfold. As a leader, do you expect your level of effectiveness to increase without raising the lid or rolling the stone away?

Sometimes, we give up on God and ourselves and assume we can never experience changes. We conclude we cannot engage the miraculous. What are your limiting thoughts and beliefs? In what ways are you restraining yourself or allowing others and things to constrain you? Are you limited more by internal or external factors? Are your feelings, resources, people, situations, things from the past, present, future, addictions or other destructive behaviors holding you back?

Our narrow perspective on life may result from childhood programming, parenting or popular culture: some of which we have not even bothered to question. Holding on to the status quo, we have come to accept this as our reality. The hope for a lid-lifting experience is unattainable because people around us are typically more willing to mourn the death of our effectiveness than encourage us to believe and act for a change.

Be determined to take the lid off your mind today.

The lid is the cap that limits your capacity to believe and have faith in your life's possibilities. If you don't have an encouraging close group that can support you to lift the lid off your effectiveness, it's time to find one! So, what's holding you back?

*Reflection*
What do you need to do to roll the stone away?

*Confession*
I declare today, "Nothing can hold me back because greater is He that is in me than he that is in the world."

*Write down the relevant practical steps you need to make the new insight a reality, and the time to implement it.*

| Practical steps | Time |
|---|---|
|  |  |

# TAKING THE STONE AWAY (2)

*Scripture Reading*

*Jesus said, "Take away the stone. Martha, the sister of the dead man, exclaimed, But Lord, by this time he [is decaying and] throws off an offensive odor, for he has been dead four days!" (John 11:39).*

*Limits, like fear, are often an illusion.*

*– Michael Jordan*

What's keeping you from taking the lid off your effectiveness or rolling the stone away? Is it fear, anxiety, doubt, shame, insecurity etc. Martha would have experienced one of these when she remarked, "By this time, Lazarus decays and throws off an offensive odor, for he has been dead four days."

Some individuals are afraid of challenging their limits. They would rather sit in their comfort zones and blame others or the system when things do not go well. They are apprehensive of what may be "lurking behind the stone." Embarrassed that they have to admit to certain self-indulgence, they would rather "keep the offensive odor at bay." In contrast, have you considered what can be if you choose to take the lid off your current capacity?

If you want to move to the next level and realize your greatness, get serious about challenging your perceived limits. Sooner or later, you will see that there are no limits except the ones we place in our own own paths. So what do you need to do?

> There are no limits except the ones we place in our own paths.

1. **PREPARATION**: Plan to confront what you may have been avoiding. Understand that fighting or denying your limits will further undermine your personal effectiveness.
2. **DECISION**: Elect to move the stone away.
3. **ACTION**: Take action to move the stone away.
4. **MOTIVE**: Be prepared for the people around who may question why you want to take the "stone" away. They may object to the reason why you need to be your best self.
5. **SHIFT**: You may disturb the equilibrium of your environment by rolling the stone away. You need to be willing to challenge the foul odor of ineffectiveness, so you can be exposed to the miracle of a new birth.
6. **RESOLUTION**: You need to contain your self-doubt. Believe and brace yourself to experience a change.
7. **PERSPECTIVE**: Is this a stone you have put in place or one people have put in place for you? The more you are exposed to an empowering influence and

atmosphere, the more you have the strength to move the stone away.

8. **DIRECTIVE**: Whose voice are you listening to? A credible leader or the popular culture?

The culture of the day may be accustomed to approaching things in a particular way. That is, when things are dead, bury it and roll a stone over it — never to come alive again. They do not see the possibility of a resurrection! However, the Master is able to bring dead things to life and sustain them with new life. The One who commands that you take away the stone is the same who has introduced Himself as the resurrection and the life.

*Reflection*
What are your limits?
Can they be addressed with faith, training, mentorship, accountability, paradigm shift, courage, discipline, commitment, hard work, perseverance etc.?

*Confession*
I roll away every limiting thoughts and beliefs today. I act valiantly.

*Write down the relevant practical steps you need to make the new insight a reality, and the time to implement it.*

| Practical steps | Time |
|---|---|
|  |  |

# IN THE DARK ROOM

*Scripture Reading*

*And [God] said to Abram, Know positively that your descendants will be strangers dwelling as temporary residents in a land that is not theirs [Egypt]. And they will be slaves there and will be afflicted and oppressed for 400 years* (Genesis 15:13).

*One who gains strength by overcoming obstacles possesses the only strength, which can overcome adversity.*

*– Albert Schweitzer*

As Abram continues with his mentor — God, He begins to reveal details of what to expect as He prepares him for greatness. He proceeded to show that greatness involves acknowledging and embracing moments of intense and chronic challenges that may bring with them immense fear, anxiety or feelings of horror.

At the moment, the experience may even seem totally contradictory to the vision or the promise received earlier from God. But stay with God and persevere; it's all in His plan. The most important point during a dark moment or challenging period of your life is to realize God is always with you. He has promised never to leave or forsake you (Deuteronomy 31:6).

In our pursuit of greatness, "all hell may break loose" on occasions. Tough moments precede great opportunities and remarkable advancement. Be encouraged to endure and persevere in great moments of persecution. They are temporary and will pass.

*Greatness involves acknowledging and embracing moments of intense and chronic challenges.*

At times, life will seem to be out of your control. You may suffer immense oppression and backlash, or you may not be rightfully compensated for your investment. Nevertheless, be diligent. Work at it. Tough moments never last but tough people do. Be resolute to overcome challenges that may come your way. The obstacle is the way!

*Reflection*
The current adversity you are experiencing has an expiry date. It will soon pass.

*Confession*
Feel free to make up and write down your confession.

*Write down the relevant practical steps you need to make the new insight a reality, and the time to implement it.*

| Practical steps | Time |
|---|---|
|  |  |

# ARE YOU READY FOR ELEVATION?

*Scripture Reading*

*And in the fourth generation they [your descendants] shall come back here [to Canaan] again, for the iniquity of the Amorities is not yet full and complete* (Genesis 15:16).

You cannot just expect a promotion to come from the sky.

*– Jesse White*

Current adversity may be a diversion to prepare you for the greatness you are about to enter. Tough situations prepare your spiritual and mental muscles to cope with the responsibilities of increase and success. Remember, muscles are developed in controlled pressure-moments.

> *You are due for a test when you are ripe for a promotion.*

Therefore, develop a mindset that always sees a negative turn of events resulting in a positive outcome. No matter what comes your way, God will always make it work out for your good (Romans 8:28). A revelation of this promise will eradicate needless anxiety and fear in your life. When a seed is planted, it undergoes a process of death before it begins to grow, blossom, and become fruitful. At times, the way to realize your dreams is to be placed in a challenging position.

Challenges are experiences that will provide you with opportunities to build relevant skills and competencies, which will come in handy when you "possess" what is rightfully yours. So have the right attitude during your perplexing times. Your products and ideas may not be well received today. In fact, they may suffer at the hands of those who may abuse or ridicule them. Nonetheless, the more an idea is fought, the stronger it becomes.

Ensure your team is clear about the vision. This prevents derailment of the dream, especially during tough challenges. Do your best to keep the vision alive in moments when it is typical to doubt the One you have trusted in the past. My friend, you are due for a test when you are ripe for a promotion or elevation. There is a flip side to every challenge — look for it! God is preparing you for a takeover bid. He is also preparing the "land" you are taking over. When the time is ripe, you will possess your possession.

*Reflection*
Who is supporting you through challenging times?
How are you supporting your team members?

*Confession*
Feel free to make up and write down your confession.

*Write down the relevant practical steps you need to make the new insight a reality, and the time to implement it.*

| Practical steps | Time |
|---|---|
|  |  |

# HOW FIT ARE YOUR MEMBERS?

*Scripture Reading*

*So now proclaim in the ears of the men, saying, Whoever is fearful and trembling, let him turn back and depart from Mount Gilead. And 22,000 of the men returned, but 10,000 remained* (Judges 7:3).

*Fitness, in my opinion, is a mental exercise more than just physical*

*– Anushka Shetty*

D uring the early stages of our organization, I was responsible for all aspects of staff recruitment and selection. Recruitment refers to the process that provides us with a pool of qualified job candidates from which to choose. Whenever there was a vacant position, we placed an advertisement that triggered a huge response from the job market. Even though the invitation is usually clear, i.e., the job role is clearly defined, most applicants who are shortlisted and

> Showing up physically does not equate to showing up psychologically.

interviewed are markedly unsuitable for the advertised role. Adding an unsuitable new member to your staff can undermine the existing chemistry and culture of your team and jeopardize the effectiveness of your organization.

Gideon had just recruited a large army for his campaign. However, he needed God to step in and conduct a screening test that determined the suitable candidates. Going into any campaign with unseasoned people may cost you dearly.

What class of people do you have on your team? Below are three classes of people who may be on your team as you make a daring move to achieve your objectives:

1. Fearful and trembling (68.75% of 32,000)
2. Tired (fatigue) and careless (97% of 10,000)
3. Battle-keen and strategy-wise (3% of 10,000)

Showing up physically does not equate to showing up psychologically. A leader requires the ability to decipher when team members respond to instructions out of duty, rather than commitment. As a parent, do you feel the emotional and relationship pulse of your children? Do they walk "on eggshells" around you? Are they paralyzed with fear whenever you are at home?

Fear creates a very unpleasant or disturbing feeling caused by the perception of an imminent and possible threat or danger. The danger might be related to a real possibility of failure, harm, injury, or loss. As a leader, are you cognizant of the physical presentation of fear or anxiety in your team members? Trembling is a physical manifestation of the fear or anxiety emotion going on inside you. Be aware of the health and emotional fitness of your team members.

*Reflection*
Do you know what drives your team members?

Why do they remain on that cause or project with you?

Do they feel coerced and browbeat to show some sort of allegiance to you or your organization?

*Confession*
Feel free to make up and write down your confession.

*Write down the relevant practical steps you need to make the new insight a reality, and the time to implement it.*

| Practical steps | Time |
|---|---|
|  |  |
|  |  |
|  |  |

# GATHER MOMENTUM

*Scripture Reading*

*That night the Lord said to Gideon, Take your father's bull, the second bull seven years old, and pull down the altar of Baal that your father has and cut down the Asherah [symbol of the goddess Asherah] that is beside it* (Judges 6:25).

*Momentum begets momentum, and the best way to start is to start.*

*– Gil Penchina*

While a myopic perspective may limit you to provide for just yourself and your family, God's intention is that you bring a global solution to the world. Why? Kingdoms expand by conquest and dominion.

After much convincing, Gideon finally took the first step of action. He conquered inertia. Like Gideon, the first person you are required to conquer is you! There is a problem you have been custom-made to address and provide a solution to. Stop debating. Start deploying.

Understand that when you begin to take your mandate seriously, people and other leaders who may have been indifferent to you in the past will rise to support you. However, it is your responsibility to generate momentum.

> Stop debating. Start deploying.

The leader's thrust determines the energy level of the team, not the other way around. Can you identify with Gideon at this juncture? Do you have any small wins under your belt? Private victories typically spark the drive to go after bigger goals. Small wins have a way of activating the determination to take on greater challenges.

Gideon conquered his inertia firstly, then his family and cultural norms, values, and programming that may have been inconsistent with his mandate. He was then poised to extend his influence by putting together a dream team that would go after the bigger prize. When leaders give a call to potential team members, clear, precise communication is essential to elicit needed momentum from budding followers.

*Reflection*

How do you measure your momentum as a team leader (parent, husband, CEO, wife)?

How can you create small wins for yourself and your team?

*Confession*
Feel free to make up and write down your confession.

*Write down the relevant practical steps you need to make the new insight a reality, and the time to implement it.*

| Practical steps | Time |
|---|---|
|  |  |

# DO IT AFRAID

*Scripture Reading*
*And the Angel of the Lord appeared to him and said to him, The Lord is with you, you mighty man of [fearless] courage* (Judges 6:12).

*If you want to conquer fear, don't sit home and think about it. Go out and get busy*

*– Dale Carnegie*

Gideon was beating wheat in the winepress to hide it from the Midianites. Like some would-be leaders, he allowed the situation he was experiencing to psychologically paralyze him. He lost faith in God, himself, and the people around him.

Things leaders who are overwhelmed with fear are unaware of:

1. **Presence**: "The Lord is with you." Gideon was unaware of God's presence and did not realize the implication of his ignorance. The presence of God is an enabler that is available to expedite the vision.

2. **Power**: Though might and power were latent in him, he failed to bring them to bear.

3. **Potential**: This leader did not view himself the way God did. He failed to recognize what God had invested in him.

In difficult situations, the first thing to acknowledge as a leader is God's presence in your life.

> Interpretation is a product of self-perception

Let this sink into your spirit and your subconscious mind. God-awareness influences the way you read and interpret a situation. Interpretation is a product of self-perception. Your self-perception determines how you deploy your potential. The release of your potential determines the power you bring to bear upon the situation.

Gideon was an example of a leader who struggled to believe God; yet, God believed in him. This is a great consolation to all those who struggle to believe God at different times. Yet, God keeps saying, "My boy, I've got you. You can do this!"

Even though we may have a glimpse of the difference we can bring to a situation, our response to the mandate is a better indicator of what is truly going on in us. Gideon attempted to judge the might and strength God invested in him by birth rank, the things on the outside, and his environment. He measured himself by opinion polls and his socioeconomic status. People err when they rely solely on what they can see physically as instrumental in making a mark in life, and fail to acknowledge — or worse — ignore the things and resources that are unseen.

What core beliefs are currently holding you back? Though afraid, Gideon did not totally allow fear to keep him from achieving his goal. He did it afraid!

*Reflection*
How many times have you failed to connect with and release the potential in you due to the limitations you have placed on yourself?

*Confession*
Even though I feel fear, I will [*insert whatever is relevant*] courageously because I know the Lord is with me.

*Write down the relevant practical steps you need to make the new insight a reality, and the time to implement it.*

| Practical steps | Time |
|-----------------|------|
|                 |      |
|                 |      |
|                 |      |

# PURPOSE FAILURE LEADS TO ABUSE

*Scripture Reading*
*But the Israelites did evil in the sight of the Lord, and the Lord gave them into the hand of Midian for seven years (Judges 6:1).*

*When people know they are created with a purpose, and not here by accident, it is life changing.*
*– Shane Harper*

When you do evil as an individual, you fail to fulfil the reason (purpose) for your position or existence. You fail to live up to your responsibilities and mandate. In other words, doing evil is synonymous with failing in your purpose and destiny. Doing evil is a choice just as doing good is a choice. The violation of your life and core principles has huge ramifications, which are usually followed by unavoidable consequences.

> You are held in bondage when you are out of sync with your purpose.

Failure to fulfil your purpose will lead to abuse. Israel did evil in the sight of the Lord. They botched their purpose and ended up being manhandled. Mike Murdoch said, "If the purpose of a thing is not known, abuse is inevitable." By extension, if you drift away from purpose, abuse is inescapable. You are held in bondage when you are out of sync with your purpose. When you are outside of purpose, you are subject to perversion or misapplication; you are forced to live in unsuitable conditions.

The following will happen when you are out of sync with your purpose:

1. **WEAKNESS:** You are forced to operate from a position of weakness. Abuse will drive and keep you away from the principal location of your calling or destiny.
2. **LABOUR:** The seed you sow (your effort and work) are at the mercy of people who can abuse them.
3. **SLAVERY:** You become subservient to the things you are designed to overcome.
4. **DYSFUCNTION:** You lead a dysfunctional lifestyle and suffer continuous abuse. You are taken advantage of and used to serve other goals. Your boundaries are decided for you and your influence is curtailed.

*Reflection*
In the sight of God, in which aspects of your life have you been engaging in evil?

What do you need to repent of?

Take time to reconnect with God now.

*Confession*
Feel free to make up and write down your confession.

*Write down the relevant practical steps you need to make the new insight a reality, and the time to implement it.*

| Practical steps | Time |
|---|---|
| | |

# FASTEST WAY TO GET NOTICED

*Scripture Reading*
*So David prevailed over the Philistine with a sling and with a stone, and struck the Philistine and slew him* (1 Samuel 17:50).

*The fastest way to gaining leadership is to be a solution provider.*

— *Lakers Komaiya*

By giving away the audio version of his book *High Performance Habits* on his newly launched podcast, #1 New York Times best-selling author and "the world's best high- performance coach" Brendon Burchard, rose to the number one spot in all categories of iTunes podcasts. His generosity with the audio version of a new book was unprecedented.

> SMART individuals deliver unusual results and get noticed.

His liberality triggered an unparalleled listener-subscription that took his podcast to the premier position.

David took the fastest route to becoming a leader. He was eager to be a solution provider by serving in a capacity no one was willing to undertake. Going by the pecking order, he was the least expected to put up his hands for the gig. However, he understood that with God on his side, he could combat the challenge those who had formal training in warfare were unwilling to confront.

There is a match between King David and Brendon Burchard's behavior. Both King David and Brendon Burchard had the willingness to:

1. Serve the people passionately
2. Undertake risks
3. Adopt an unusual approach
4. Lead when others thought they were crazy
5. Be willing to be misunderstood
6. Be perceived as underdogs.
7. Add value to the people they serve

In a world where mediocre and average results are the order of the day, **SMART** individuals deliver unusual results and get noticed fast. Do you invest in **S**elf-Mastery? Are you **M**otivated? Are you **A**udacious? Are you **R**elentless in your pursuit of excellence and serving others? Are you **T**otally focused? Like David, be a leader who gets the attention of others, not by mere talk but by your action.

*Reflection*
Are you a **SMART** leader?

Which aspect of being **SMART** do you need to work on?

*Confession*
Feel free to make up and write down your confession.

*Write down the relevant practical steps you need to make the new insight a reality, and the time to implement it.*

| Practical steps | Time |
| --- | --- |
|  |  |

# WHEN YOU NEED TO CALL A FOUL

*Scripture Reading*

*For rebellion is as the sin of witchcraft, and stubbornness is as idolatry and teraphim (household good luck images). Because you have rejected the word of the Lord, He also has rejected you from being king* (1 Samuel 15:23).

*We love a tale of heroes and villains and conflicts requiring a neat resolution.*

*– Barry Ritholtz*

God kicked King Saul out of His organization. Remember, the one who makes you can break you. The corollary also is "If they didn't make you, they can't break you." People may be disqualified from their positions for two major reasons:

> *You need to provide psychological safety before initiating a difficult conversation.*

1. Rebellion (total refusal to follow a leader, as well as the principles and values he stands for)
2. Disobedience

Intentional leaders are willing to have difficult conversations with the people on their teams. In this case, Samuel was willing to call the "foul" on King Saul. Saul had infringed on a core value of the organization: obedience.

Even though Samuel mourned all night over God's rejection of Saul, when he approached Saul to broach the topic, he reined his emotion in. This suggests that you should provide psychological safety before initiating a difficult conversation. Psychological safety is present when people feel safe to take risks and be vulnerable with each other. Then you can proceed thus:

1. Put your conversation in context
2. Proceed with facts
3. Recount what the expectations were
4. Highlight the deviation from the expectations
5. Give a chance and listen to the defense of the individual
6. Treat the person with respect
7. Acknowledge the individual's argument
8. Explain the consequences of the person's actions
9. Provide a save-face moment for the individual
10. Allow yourself and the other individual to express healthy emotions

Conflict management is hardly an easy task, but one you need to master as a leader.

*Reflection*
What crucial conversation have you been avoiding having with one of the people on your team?

*Confession*
Feel free to make up and write down your confession.

*Write down the relevant practical steps you need to make the new insight a reality, and the time to implement it.*

| Practical steps | Time |
| --- | --- |
|  |  |

# PREPARE TO GET NOTICED

*Scripture Reading*

*One of the young men said, I have seen a son of Jesse the Bethlehemite who plays skilfully, a valiant man, a man of war, prudent in speech and eloquent, an attractive person; and the Lord is with him* (1 Samuel 16:18).

*Success is where opportunity meets preparation.*
*– Bobby Unser*

Remember David, at this stage, was a shepherd boy tending sheep in the backside of the wilderness. On recommendation, Saul requested David from Jesse as "your son, who is with the sheep." After David was anointed, the next step was to make him visible to someone who mattered. Thus, providing the passage for his appointment. This pathway led to David solving a problem — whenever he played his lyre, Saul was refreshed, became well, and relieved of a distressing condition. As I remarked earlier, the fastest way to gaining leadership is to become a solution provider.

Challenges are opportunities in work clothes. You have to learn to love work. Quite a number of people struggle with those two words (love and work), especially when they come after each other. I want you to embrace challenges because every piece of work you do has the potential to align you with someone who matters and needs a solution. Put your best in whatever you do today. Be excellent at what is good. Be innocent of evil (Romans 16:19).

David was not excellent at what he did because he was waiting to be introduced to King Saul. He simply did what he had to do. He performed his duties and responsibilities excellently.

> You have to learn to love work and court challenges.

Tom Waits said, "The way you do anything is the way you do everything." David made himself visible. He engaged. He connected.

Relentless in service, David began to rise through the ranks — from serving his father to serving King Saul, from tending sheep to becoming Saul's demon-chaser and armor-bearer. You need to understand that no matter how crowded the environment; your gift will always create room for you. From going back and forth before Saul, David soon earned himself the opportunity to remain in Saul's service.

*Reflection*
What are you working on or preparing excellently that will catch the eyes of someone who matters?

*Confession*

Feel free to make up and write down your confession.

*Write down the relevant practical steps you need to make the new insight a reality, and the time to implement it.*

| Practical steps | Time |
|---|---|
|  |  |

# PREPARING TO GET NOTICED

*Scripture Reading*

*One of the young men said, I have seen a son of Jesse the Bethlehemite who plays skilfully, a valiant man, a man of war, prudent in speech and eloquent, an attractive person; and the Lord is with him* (1 Samuel 16:18).

Nothing is more expensive than a missed opportunity.

*– H. Jackson Brown, Jr.*

I want you to take a closer look at the scripture we focused on yesterday. Embedded in it are top qualities you need to consistently work on to get noticed and bring your gifting, talents, and expertise to people who matter.

1. **POTENTIAL:** "A son" indicates youthfulness, agility, flexibility, willingness, and readiness to serve.
2. **PROFICIENCY:** "Plays skilfully" indicates discipline, commitment to practice, and teachability.
3. **PERSEVERANCE:** "Valiant man" indicates possession of courage and determination of purpose.

4. **PROWESS**: "Man of war" indicates boldness, audacity, and readiness to contend for values and principles. One with leadership ability to organize and coordinate troops for war. You may have the boldness to enter a tough situation, but not have the courage to persevere. To be noticed, you need both.

> *You may have boldness to enter a tough situation, but not have the courage to persevere.*

5. **PROPAGATION**: "Prudent in speech and eloquent" indicates an excellent communicator with exceptional relational skills.

6. **PERSONALITY**: "Attractive person" indicates attention to personal grooming and presentation, loveable personality, and excellent character.

7. **PRESENCE**: "The Lord is with him" indicates the extra factor, acknowledgment of God's presence, depends on or allows God to make up for whatever he/she lacks.

*Reflection*

Out of these seven qualities, which ones would you currently rate as your strengths and which ones would you rate as your weaknesses?

What can you do to invigorate your strengths and weaknesses?

*Confession*

Feel free to make up and write down your confession.

*Write down the relevant practical steps you need to make the new insight a reality, and the time to implement it.*

| Practical steps | Time |
| --- | --- |
|  |  |
|  |  |
|  |  |
|  |  |

# WHO IS YOUR ROLE MODEL?

*Scripture Reading*

*When they had come, he looked on Eliab [the eldest son] and said, Surely the Lord's anointed is before Him. But the Lord said to Samuel, Look not on his appearance or at the heights of his stature, for I have rejected him, For the Lord sees not as man sees, for man looks on the outward appearance, but the Lord looks on the heart* (1 Samuel 16: 6-7).

*You've got to be careful whom you pattern yourself after because you're likely to become just like them.*
*– Rich Mayo*

What did King Saul and Eliab have in common? God rejected the former after he had a shot at leading; the latter was not even given a shot, he was disqualified! The Scripture records that Eliab and his two other

> *What leaders am I keeping company with? Who is mentoring me?*

brothers earlier decided to follow Saul as soldiers in the

king's army. Can two walk together unless they are agreed?

Some pertinent questions you can consider today are:

1. What leaders am I keeping company with?
2. Who is mentoring me?
3. Was Eliab disqualified because of his association with Saul, his leader?

You can be invalidated because of those you follow. David served Saul but did not follow in his footsteps. He followed Saul as a positional leader. John Maxwell defined this as the lowest level of leadership. Saul had a title but did not invest in his own growth and development. He relied on his position to get people to follow him.

After Saul's appointment, he became more concerned with his public image and people's opinions of him. Although he displayed a spark of capacity to lead, he ultimately failed to develop his potential and capabilities. Hence, he could not move to the next level of leadership. The Scripture records that Caleb wholly followed the Lord spiritually, intellectually, and psychologically. He aligned his thoughts with God's thoughts and his ways (behavior) with God's way of acting.

Jesus is the perfect example of a person who became one with God. He did exactly what He was shown and followed instructions promptly and expressly. He decreased, while God increased. Leaders who want to follow in the footsteps of Jesus do so in times of clarity and confusion, plenty and lack, peace and war, when approved by men or otherwise.

*Reflection*
As a leader, what qualities do you look for when you scout for a mentor?

*Confession*
Feel free to make up and write down your confession.

*Write down the relevant practical steps you need to make the new insight a reality, and the time to implement it.*

| Practical steps | Time |
|---|---|
|  |  |
|  |  |
|  |  |
|  |  |

# AGREE TO DISAGREE

*Scripture Reading:*
*Therefore, My brethren, whom I love and yearn to see,*
*my delight and crown (wreath of victory), thus stand*
*firm in the Lord, my beloved. I entreat and advise Euodia*
*and I entreat and advise Syntyche to agree and to work*
*in harmony in the Lord* (Philippians 4:1-2).

*If everyone is moving forward together, then success*
*takes care of itself.*

*– Henry Ford*

How do you as a leader, parent, manager, supervisor or an elder manage conflict or disagreement among the individuals you oversee? True leaders encourage synergy. They build enabling organizational cultures that foster unity and teamwork.

Consider why people may find it difficult to work together:

1. Different mindsets and values

2. Differences in opinions and goals
3. Differing personalities

I have observed the key ingredient that makes a relationship work is the agreement to work — whether

> *The key ingredient that makes a relationship work is the agreement to work.*

it is in an organization, a marriage, or a business relationship. An agreement is often based on shared values and a subscription to the "big picture." Further, the indication of an agreement is working together in harmony.

A four-part choral group typically has a treble, alto, tenor, and bass singers. Each member of each part of the choir sings at a slightly different frequency and tone. The different tone, however, blends together to create what in music is referred to as harmony. Harmony does not mean you have to work and see things from the same point of view. What's crucial is that your "different" point of view is beneficial to the organization helping it to achieve its core objectives and goals.

*Reflection:*

As a leader, do you struggle to work with people who share different opinions to yours?

Do you lose focus of the big picture, hence, become self-centered and tunnel-visioned?

*Confession*
Feel free to make up and write down your confession.

*Write down the relevant practical steps you need to make the new insight a reality, and the time to implement it.*

| Practical steps | Time |
| --- | --- |
|  |  |

# BEST PROMISE EVER

*Scripture Reading*
*No man shall be able to stand before you all the days of your life. As I was with Moses, so I will be with you; I will not fail you or forsake you* (Joshua 1:5).

*Life takes on meaning when you become motivated, set goals and charge after them in an unstoppable manner.*
*– Les Brown*

When you realize the power in collaboration, you become excited about forming alliances with people you can serve but who can also add value to you. Joshua had just received a commission from God to prepare to lead his team and extend their dominance. However, God made it clear to him that his domain had boundaries. You are not called to divert your energy in a million and one directions but to focus on your particular area of influence.

> If you ally with God, you become unstoppable.

To achieve this, God gave Joshua the best promise ever. In other words, He assured Joshua that he would have access to all that God is: to the extent that NO man shall be able to withstand Joshua in all his campaigns all the days of his life. God seems to say to Joshua as He is saying to you now, "If you ally with Me, you will become unstoppable." He is your Source and He commands the best resources.

Please understand that this assurance does not mean men (who will surely throw obstacles at you) will not come against you. Indeed, they will attempt to stand in your way. Nevertheless, they will ultimately be deprived of their abilities to engage you long-term and overcome you. You may encounter adversity, but you will come out on top. So be confident and of good courage during the process. I always remind myself that an audacious mindset leads to confident practices and behaviors.

*Reflection*

As a leader, what does it mean to have God mentor you in your field of endeavor?

How are you going about seeking the best mentors in your field?

*Confession*

Feel free to make up and write down your confession.

*Write down the relevant practical steps you need to make the new insight a reality, and the time to implement it.*

| Practical steps | Time |
|---|---|
|  |  |

# WHAT'S YOUR SELF-TALK?

*Scripture Reading*
*For she kept saying to herself, "If I only touch His garment, I shall be restored to health"* (Matthew 9:21).

*Don't be a victim of negative self-talk. Remember you are listening.*

*– Bob Proctor*

Y ou may deceive others but eventually, your life-outcome will be evident to all, which is a true reflection of what you have been saying to yourself. Are you aware of the narrative you have been rehashing to yourself? Ultimately, you tend to believe your own story more than what anyone is attempting to tell you.

> *Always meditate on a bank of scriptures that will motivate you to achieve your goals and dreams.*

I want to encourage you to always meditate on a bank of scriptures or proclamations that will motivate you to achieve your goals and dreams. Ensure to replace doubt and negative thoughts with positive ones. Feed on empowering content and literature. Listen to enriching podcasts and uplifting music. Watch movies that will open your mind and spirit to a new vista of hope and possibilities. Remember, what you focus on and expose yourself to largely influence what you keep saying to yourself.

I have noticed that people usually stop saying narratives to themselves that may have been potent in the past when:

1. Things are not happening the **WAY** they want them to
2. Things are not happening in the **TIME** they want them to
3. Things are not happening to the **DEGREE** they want them to
4. Things are not happening in the **ORDER** in which they want them to

For you to achieve your objectives, you need to create a clear mental picture of your goals, reinforced by a positive narrative. Then, take congruent action steps in the direction of your vision. This is one of the secrets of sustained and progressive success.

*Reflection*
What do you tell yourself especially in times of lack, loss, adversity, challenge, doubt, pain, conflict, and need?

Are you aware of the story you keep telling yourself in your mind?

Is it empowering or disempowering?

*Confession*
Feel free to make up and write down your confession.

*Write down the relevant practical steps you need to make the new insight a reality, and the time to implement it.*

| Practical steps | Time |
|---|---|
|  |  |

# MENTORS MODEL MESSAGE

*Scripture Reading*
*I give you a new commandment: that you should love one another. Just as I have loved you, so you too should love one another* (John 13:34).

*Love begins by taking care of the closest ones – the ones at home.*

*– Mother Teresa*

It is important to know the defining features your organization and other team members should reflect. In this sense, you cannot be all things to all men. Further, you cannot ask of your team members what you have not modeled to them.

At times, we ask of people what we are not able or willing to give. In particular, some people demand commitment when they have not even invested in doing the hard yards. People, however, tend to "do as you do and not as

> Given an enabling environment, most things in life can be learned and developed over time.

you say." Consequently, these kinds of leaders produce team members who have flippant attitudes towards the organizational objectives.

Leaders who have truly considered the requirements of a task or activity and have modeled this can confidently demand the same of team members. Great leaders understand that given an enabling environment, most things in life can be learned and developed over time. Leaders set the tone for how team members treat and relate to each other.

Have you asked yourself lately what you are communicating to your team members, family members, and tribe members? If someone demands one of your team members to say what your organizational culture is, what would be the person's response? Will your team member struggle to articulate this? Remember, it is important to connect, communicate, and model *lead* values to those you lead.

*Reflection*
Who are your team members and what are you modeling to them?

*Confession*
Feel free to make up and write down your confession.

*Write down the relevant practical steps you need to make the new insight a reality, and the time to implement it.*

| Practical steps | Time |
|---|---|
|  |  |

# LESSON 30
# WHAT'S STANDING IN YOUR WAY?

*Scripture Reading*

*And behold, a woman who had suffered from a flow a blood for twelve years came up behind Him and touched the fringe of His garment* (Matthew 9:20).

*Growth is painful. Change is painful. But nothing is as painful as staying stuck where you do not belong.*
*– N. R. Narayana Murthy*

H ave you come to a point in your leadership journey where you are in a rut or you perceive the current challenge facing you is insurmountable? Consider the seven things the woman in the scripture reading did not permit to stand in the way of her personal healing, growth, and development.

> *Faith is grounded in a decision to connect with someone who can make a difference in your life.*

1. **TRAUMA**: The woman's haemorrhagic condition would have been a perfect alibi for her not to

intentionally access the One who could bring about a change in her life. How often do you justify the rut you have found yourself in because of an unfavorable incident that occurred?

2. **PHYSICAL** factor: Physical weakness from excessive loss of blood could have kept her from overcoming inertia.

3. The **PAST**: Past failure and unsuccessful attempts at getting cured could have posed a barrier to seeking the Master's touch. How often do you consider failure to be final?

4. The **ENVIRONMENT**: Heaps of people trying to get Jesus' attention or simply catch a glimpse of Him posed an overwhelming obstacle to her. Sadly, most of these people were just spectators who simply came to see the "show."

5. The **CULTURE**: In those days, haemorrhaging women were considered unclean. They were not allowed to touch things or people considered clean or consecrated to God. The woman risked being censored by the powers that be of that era.

6. **SELF-DOUBT**: She had to overcome this by constantly saying to herself, "If I only touch His garment, I shall be restored to health."

7. **SHAME**: The scripture notes that "She came up behind Him." This suggests that she may have been ridden with indignity and humiliation as she approached Jesus for healing.

Jesus promptly recognized all that this woman did not permit to stand in her way and commented that her faith made her whole. Her faith was grounded in the decision to connect with someone who could turn her life around. Change starts the moment an internal decision is made. However, it may take commitment to process and time for the outcome to be made manifest.

*Reflection*
Who are your team members and what are you modeling to them?

*Confession*
Feel free to make up and write down your confession.

*Write down the relevant practical steps you need to make the new insight a reality, and the time to implement it.*

| Practical steps | Time |
| --- | --- |
|  |  |

# COMMITMENT TO CHANGE

*Scripture Reading*
*And behold, a woman who had suffered from a flow a blood for twelve years came up behind Him and touched the fringe of His garment* (Matthew 9:20).

*Dreams are the seeds of change. Nothing ever grows without a seed, and nothing ever changes without a dream.*

*– Debby Boone*

I encounter people daily who attempt to convince me that they are simply victims of situations they never initiated. Hence, they are powerless to effect any changes. Some give reasons they believe are legitimate; others appear to have simply perfected the "blame game."

> *Some people will rather define themselves by the pain they experience than commit to a process that may help them accept what they cannot change.*

A common feature of these two groups, however, is that they would rather define themselves by the pain and suffering they experience than commit to any process that may help them to willfully accept what they are unable to change and commit to what they can.

In speaking to and surveying leaders in different domains of life, I observed that they have attitudes similar to the woman described in today's scripture reading:

1. Leaders rise above pain, suffering, and tragedy. They refuse to be defined by past or current situations.
2. They orient themselves towards the vision of the future. Even though mindful of the present, the focus on the prize they strive for helps them to sustain the momentum required to keep them moving in the direction of their goals.
3. They are relentless individuals. They are not the type that will give up. Rather, they have the attitude that says, "If you see me fighting in the forest with a grizzly bear, help the bear."
4. They create a mental image and permit themselves to be driven by it.
5. According to Pastor Bill Hybel, they have a "bias towards action." They understand that faith without works is dead (James 2:17).

To develop the greatness within, not only do you need to be a change agent, it is essential you use "change" to the best of your advantage.

# COMMITMENT TO CHANGE

*Reflection*

What vision have you seen that you are committedly working towards to bring about its realization?

*Confession*

Feel free to make up and write down your confession.

*Write down the relevant practical steps you need to make the new insight a reality, and the time to implement it.*

| Practical steps | Time |
|---|---|
|  |  |

# MAKE THE BIG ASK

*Scripture Reading*

*As Jesus passed on from there, He saw a man named Matthew sitting at the tax collector's office; and He said to him, Be My disciple (side with My party and follow Me). And he rose and followed Him* (Matthew 9:9).

*So I say to you, Ask and it will be given to you; search, and you will find; knock, and the door will be opened for you.*

*– Jesus Christ*

Intentional leaders use stellar moments to motivate potential team members to make the "big ask." Concerning enlisting people to join your team who will bring about your vision, Bill Hybels, author of *Axiom* wrote, "I realized long ago that 'asking' would always be a significant part of my leadership role. What I didn't know was that the longer I led, the bigger my 'asks' would get."

> *People don't care what you know until they know that you care.*

You may be one of those people who still struggle to ask for help or to enrol people to join you in a worthy cause. One of the often-cited reasons most individuals give for this is the fear of rejection. My experience is that if the big ask is well-timed and presented, people actually feel honored to help and advance your cause. This is especially so if you are seen as a person who cares about people, not just things (or your things).

A couple of points to note when you are making the "big ask":

1.  Be clear about **what you are asking**. Whenever I approach people for any kind of support, I'm specific about exactly what I need from them: to complete a task, to serve in a particular capacity, to provide resources or to leverage their influence.

2.  Be clear about **what the person you are asking will benefit**. Mentors and coaches continue to be relevant in our lives because experience has shown that we all want to be part of something great or, even more, live a life of impact. Help people understand you care about them and are willing to help them meet their needs. It has been said, "People don't care what you know until they know that you care."

3.  Be clear about **what you want them to do**. This is often referred to as a "call to action." Let them understand what "action" looks like. Avoid the ambiguity that may result from the person mentally consenting to your demand but not knowing how to actively respond to your "big ask."

4. Make them feel and **let them know you care about their success**. Les Brown once said, "Help people achieve their dreams, and you will achieve yours."

No one is able to achieve great things on his/her own. A leader cannot operate as a solo enterprise. Jesus started by preaching, teaching, and healing the sick. As time went on, He needed to make the "big ask" to get people to buy-in to His vision so he could make a greater impact.

*Reflection*
What "big ask" have you been willing to make but have been procrastinating on?

*Confession*
Feel free to make up and write down your own confession.

*Write down the relevant practical steps you need to make the new insight a reality, and the time to implement it.*

| Practical steps | Time |
|---|---|
|  |  |

# WHO ARE YOU CALLED TO SERVE?

*Scripture Reading*

*And when the Pharisees saw this, they said to His disciples, "Why does your Master eat with tax collectors and those (pre-eminently) sinful?" But when Jesus heard it, He replied, "Those who are strong and well (healthy) have no need of a physician, but those who are weak and sick"* (Matthew 9:11-11).

*The aim of marketing is to know and understand the customer so well the product or service fits him and sells itself.*

*– Peter Drucker*

The Bible records, in Matthew 1:21 that Mary would bring forth a Son and His name would be called Jesus because He would save His people from their sins. In spite of this,

> *You cannot afford to be unclear about the demographics you are called to serve.*

the Pharisees were confused as to the ones who needed Jesus' service the most.

You cannot afford to be unclear about the demographics you are called to serve. I believe it is possible to serve but serve the wrong crowd. Do you really know the people who need your A-game the most? Are you aware of the people who buy your products or services? Jesus made it clear that He won't be spending valuable time and resources with those who do not need His offering. He insisted that He came to add value to those who require His provisions and appreciate them.

Intentional leaders understand the needs of the people they have been called to serve and use the right strategies to qualify, attract, and connect with the right following. Furthermore, they know the solutions their offerings will provide their target audiences. Hence, they understand the necessity of bringing their A-game on. A progressive knowledge and understanding of your demographics is an activity to which you need to devote time. This is significant because any attempt to qualify the wrong crowd will result in a waste of valuable resources.

So how do you get your audience to have a changed mindset about your offering? By highlighting:

1. **Cost of inaction**: Letting them know the price of remaining in their status quo or their comfort zones.
2. **Solution**: Letting them know the specific need your offering will meet.
3. **Joy**: Helping them create a visual image of how better their lives will be with the solution.

*Reflection*
What are the distinguishing features of your key audience? Where can you find them? What are their needs? How can your offerings solve their problems?

*Confession*
Feel free to make up and write down your confession.

*Write down the relevant practical steps you need to make the new insight a reality, and the time to implement it.*

| Practical steps | Time |
|---|---|
| | |
| | |
| | |
| | |
| | |

# BUILT TO LAST

*Scripture Reading*

*So everyone who hears these words of Mine and acts upon them (obeying them) will be like a sensible (prudent, practical, wise) man who built his house upon the rock* (Matthew 7:24).

*Have a bias toward action - let's see something happen now. You can break that big plan into small steps and take the first step right away.*

*– Indira Ghandi*

Business leaders are not in control of the "rain, the flood, and the wind" in their situations. This is similar to how factors such as market forces and competitors' strategies are outside of their control. However, what they can influence is their commitment to discipline and right action. Zig Ziglar once remarked, "It was character that got us out of bed, commitment that moved

> *How much of what I know am I putting into action?*

us into action, and discipline that enabled us to follow through."

Commitment to sound leadership and business principles typically puts a leader in a vantage position. Ed Louis Cole said, "Every man is limited by the knowledge in his mind, the strength of his character, and the principle upon which he is building his life." One of the steps to overcoming these limitations is by taking action to update your knowledge, work on the weak links in your character set, and continuously testing and reviewing the standards you hold yourself to in life.

In other words, it's not enough to move from one seminar to another, to consume pages of books or listen to several podcasts. The question you always need to ask yourself is, "How much of what I know am I putting into action?"

Action indicates obedience. Hence, every act of obedience can be compared to a progressive contribution to the erection of a solid structure situated on a stable foundation. One of the challenges that often stand in the way of followers is inaction, especially in transiting from being mere consumers of information to "doers" who live the reality of the new evidence they have found. If you want "built-to-last," you have to be sensible enough to follow the precise instructions of your Mentor and mentors.

*Reflection*
What information have you recently gleaned that you are yet to put into action?

What do you need to do to move from a consumer of information to one who digests and becomes a "doer"?

*Confession*
Feel free to make up and write down your confession.

*Write down the relevant practical steps you need to make the new insight a reality, and the time to implement it.*

| Practical steps | Time |
|---|---|
|  |  |

# WHO IS YOUR LEADER FOLLOWING?

*Scripture Reading*
*Every tree that does not bear good fruit is cut down and cast into the fire. Therefore, you will fully know them by their fruits* (Matthew 7:19-20).

*I think there is probably no better person to aspire to emulate than Steve Jobs and what he has done at Apple in terms of his leadership, his innovation, not settling for mediocrity.*

*– Howard Schultz*

Even though gardening has never been my area of strength, I recognize that if you want oranges, you need to plant orange seeds, not lemon. My research and observation show that some people get behind leaders based on the shallow promises they offer and not on actual past or current outcomes. This is even more common in environments where followers are hypnotised by a leader's charisma over his/her character and competence.

Before you rally behind a leader, do your due diligence. Ask the person or research who he/she follows, as well as what the person's "true" character and past achievements are. Don't just take the person's word for it; check out his/her "fruits." Are these leaders living their talk? Leaders who are devouring wolves dressed as sheep are pretenders. They misguide people. They are like salesmen who do not personally use their products or services. They are not who they present themselves to be. They misrepresent. In spite of what false leaders profess, when the seed in them eventually produces, they are seen for who they truly are.

> *Leaders who endorse mediocrity set a limiting bar for the people who may follow them.*

People, however, trust leaders who bear fruit consistent with what they confess. Smart followers relate to leaders, not just based on charisma but on outcomes. Understand that as a leader, people owe it to themselves to do due diligence on you before they commit to the vision you share with them. Leaders who endorse mediocrity set a limiting bar for the people who may follow them. This is an extension of John C. Maxwell's "Law of the Lid," which states, "Leadership ability is the lid that determines a person's level of effectiveness. The lower an individual's ability to lead, the lower the lid on his potential." Therefore, as a leader, be wise in selecting mentors and other leaders you collaborate with. As a follower, exercise sound judgment as you seek to commit to the vision of a potential leader.

*Reflection*

In which areas of your life do you think you "talk" more than you "do"?

What can you begin to do to bridge the gap?

*Confession*

Feel free to make up and write down your own confession.

*Write down the relevant practical steps you need to make the new insight a reality, and the time to implement it.*

| Practical steps | Time |
|-----------------|------|
|                 |      |

# THREE THINGS NOT TO DO AS LEADERS

*Scripture Reading*

*Do not judge and criticise and condemn others, so that you may not be judged and criticised and condemned yourselves* (Matthew 7:1).

*Condemn none. If you can stretch out a helping hand, do so. If you cannot, fold your hands, bless your brothers, and let them go their own way.*

*– Swami Vivekananda*

Most people are prone to provide their opinions on issues — leaders especially. May I suggest three things you should avoid in this process because of the influence you have over people?

1. **Judge**: Give unfavorable or negative evaluation of others without giving an indication of how they can improve. In addition, it is more empowering to address the behavior and action of a person than their "person." When you fuse or equate the person with the bad or negative behavior, you suggest the

individual is inherently incapable of making the changes necessary. Rather than judge, empathize, encourage, and infuse strength in the people you lead.

2. **Criticise**: Find fault with or point out real or perceived defects or flaws. Real leaders are given to developing people. They are "strength-finders" rather than "fault-finders." Instead of criticising, critique and bring out the best in your followers. Emphasize their strengths and talents, and inspire them to work on their weaknesses.

3. **Condemn**: Dismiss or declare as unfit, express a strong disapproval of. Rather than condemn, provide an opportunity for them to hope again or bounce back from adversity.

It can be said that it is easier to judge others by their actions, while we assess ourselves by our intentions. In other words, we refuse to use equal weights in our evaluation of others and ourselves. We forget to apply the Golden Rule: Do to others what you would have them do to you (Matthew 7:12).

> *It is easier to judge others by their actions, while we assess ourselves by our intentions.*

Determine beforehand how you want people to relate to you and then treat them the same way. Give and it shall be given to you (Luke 6:38).

It is a good practice to always consider the motives and intentions behind your evaluation of your team member. Ask yourself, "Is it to build up or to destroy?"

*Reflection*
Which of these three: judge, criticize or condemn are you most prone to when dealing with team members?

Reflect on what you need to do to encourage and build people up.

*Confession*
Feel free to make up and write down your confession.

*Write down the relevant practical steps you need to make the new insight a reality, and the time to implement it.*

| Practical steps | Time |
|---|---|
|  |  |

# GIVING FEEDBACK

*Scripture Reading*

*Why do you stare from without at the very small particle that is in your brother's eye but do not become aware of consider the beam of timber that is in your eye?* (Matthew 7:3).

*I think it's very important to have a feedback loop, where you're constantly thinking about what you've done and how you could be doing it better.*

*– Elon Musk*

As you work on developing the greatness within you, you will need to cultivate the essential skills of providing feedback to people you work with. This becomes relevant because your team needs to know how they are doing with regards to achieving the goals of the organization. They need to know if their performances are in line with your expectations. They need to learn what they have done well and what they need to improve. Traditionally, this information has been communicated in the form of "downward feedback" from leaders to the team members. Just as the people you lead need feedback, you will also benefit from the feedback your team members give you.

As I reflected on the Golden Rule that stipulates, "Do to others as you would have them do to you," a line of thought occurred to me. What if you are used to deprecating yourself, hence, you find it acceptable to demean others because that is what you expect from them? It may be customary for you to negatively evaluate others since you do not know any better. However, the point here is that the starting premise is faulty. A leader who has a lot of adjustments to make in various areas of life will find it challenging to provide quality and positive feedback to team members.

Whether you are a parent, a coach or an executive at any level, do not be preoccupied with the inadequacies of the people you lead at the expense of making conscious efforts to address the palpable weaknesses in your personal or professional life. Don't be the type of leader that externalizes his/her shortcomings on team members to divert attention from vital self-evaluation and development. Don't leave the "beam of timber in your eyes" while straining to remove the speck in the eye of your team member (Matthew 7:3). The more effective you are at tackling the things in your blind spot, the better you are at providing valuable critique to the people you lead.

> *Don't leave the beam in your eyes while straining to remove the speck in the eye of another.*

*Reflection*

If you were to be evaluated by the feedback you provide, how would you fare?

Are you authentic enough to deliver the feedback?

*Confession*

Feel free to make up and write down your confession.

*Write down the relevant practical steps you need to make the new insight a reality, and the time to implement it.*

| Practical steps | Time |
|---|---|
|  |  |

# FEEDFORWARD

*Scripture Reading*
*Why do you stare from without at the very small particle that is in your brother's eye but do not become aware of consider the beam of timber that is in your eye?* (Matthew 7:3).

*We all need people who will give us feedback. That's how we improve.*

*– Bill Gates*

A s a leader, giving quality feedback can often be challenging even at the best of times. This is so because feedback is phrased in the context of some inadequacy that occurred in the past. Marshall Goldsmith, in his article titled, "Try feedforward instead of feedback" noted, "There is a fundamental problem with all types of feedback: it focuses on a past, on what

> *The feedforward notion offers suggestions that might help people achieve a positive change in their selected behaviors.*

has already occurred — not on the infinite variety of opportunities that can happen in the future. As much, feedback can be limited and static as opposed to expansive and dynamic." He described the feedforward notion as suggestions for the future that might help team members achieve positive changes in their selected behaviors.

Some of the reasons for adopting a feedforward concept in a review process are:

1. We can change the future. We can't change the past. Feedforward helps people envision and focus on a positive future, not a failed past. Athletes are often trained using feedforward. Basketball players are taught to envision the ball going into the hoop and to imagine the perfect shot.

2. It can be more productive to help people be "right," than prove they were "wrong." Negative feedback often becomes an exercise in "Let me prove you were wrong." This tends to produce defensiveness on the part of the receiver and discomfort on the part of the sender.

3. Feedforward is especially suited to successful people. Successful people like getting ideas that are aimed at helping them achieve their goals. They tend to resist negative judgment. We all tend to accept feedback that is consistent with the way we see ourselves. We also tend to reject or deny feedback that is

inconsistent with the way we see ourselves. Successful people tend to have a very positive self-image.

4. People do not take feedforward as personally as feedback. In theory, constructive feedback is supposed to "focus on the performance, not the person." In practice, almost all feedback is taken personally (no matter how it is delivered). Successful people's sense of identity is highly connected with their work. The more successful people are, the more this tends to be true. It is hard to give a dedicated professional feedback that is not taken personally. Feedforward cannot involve a personal critique, since it is discussing something that has not yet happened! Positive suggestions tend to be seen as objective advice — personal critiques are often viewed as personal attacks.

5. Feedforward can cover almost all of the same "material" as feedback.

6. People tend to listen more attentively to feedforward than feedback. One participant in the feedforward exercise noted, "I think that I listened more effectively in this exercise than I ever do at work!" When asked why, he responded, "Normally, when others are speaking, I am so busy composing a reply that will make sure I sound smart that I am not fully listening to what the other person is saying. In

feedforward the only reply I am allowed to make is 'thank you.' Since I don't have to worry about composing a clever reply, I can focus all of my energy on listening to the other person!"

*Reflection*

If you were at the receiving end of a feedforward review, how would you feel at the end of the session?

*Confession*

Feel free to make up and write down your confession.

*Write down the relevant practical steps you need to make the new insight a reality, and the time to implement it.*

| Practical steps | Time |
|---|---|
|  |  |

# THE RELENTLESS LEADER

*Scripture Reading*

*For everyone who keeps asking receives; and he who keeps on seeking finds; and to him who keeps on knocking, [the door] will be opened* (Matthew 7:8).

*Being relentless means craving the end result so intensely that the work becomes irrelevant.*

*– Tim Grover*

Our success or failure lies in what we commit ourselves to do on a daily basis. Denzel Washington once said, "Without commitment, you'll never start. Without consistency you'll never finish." To check how you rate on the relentless meter, reflect on and answer the following questions:

1. To what practices have you unswervingly dedicated yourself to improve your odds of success in life?
2. When was the last time you reflected on whether you have been asking the right questions in your field of endeavor?

3. Are you devoted to seeking solutions to meaningful problems?
4. Are you using or leveraging the right tools to explore?
5. Are you improving in serving your customers faster or better?
6. Are you knocking on the right door to provide value-added products and services?
7. Are you looking into how you can extend your service provision?

The scripture reading today suggests clear outcomes for specific initiatives. In other words, if you keep asking, you receive. If you keep seeking, you find. If you keep knocking, the door will be opened.

Even though everyone has been offered these promises, the vast majority does not take advantage of them. Arguably, people fail to benefit because most lack the discipline to persevere. Research and experience have shown me that one of the key virtues of bringing dreams to reality is persistence. Great leaders seem to always leverage the staying power others have failed to develop.

> *People fail to benefit because most lack the discipline to persevere.*

*Reflection*

What may be preventing you from benefiting from the promises in Matthew 7:8?

*Confession*
Feel free to make up and write down your confession.

*Write down the relevant practical steps you need to make the new insight a reality, and the time to implement it.*

| Practical steps | Time |
|---|---|
|  |  |

# ROADBLOCKS ON RELENTLESS STREET

*Scripture Reading*

*For everyone who keeps asking receives; and he who keeps on seeking finds; and to him who keeps on knocking, [the door] will be opened* (Matthew 7:8)

*I've known lots of people that are talented and nothing happens. It's not about talent, it is about a relentless drive.*

*– Julie Brown*

One of the staggering realities I have come to appreciate is that creativity, gifts, and talents do not guarantee success. I have repeatedly come across people with amazing skills and dexterity that have not been able to convert their giftedness to anything remarkable.

Let me suggest some roadblocks that these individuals allow to stand in their way:

1. Failure to **remain strong**. This manifests in the form of fatigue. They fail to maintain mental and physical stamina.
2. Failure to **persevere**: This is more so in an era where people subscribe to being so fast-paced that they are impatient to get anything worthwhile.
3. Failure to **believe or continue in faith** — doubt
4. Failure to **maintain focus** — distraction
5. Failure to **acknowledge God's providence** — scarcity
6. Failure to **understand** — dullness of mind
7. Failure to **engage purpose** — lack of meaning

It's time to recalibrate yourself by asking the questions that will get you out of the rut even if self-reflection becomes confronting and takes you out of your comfort zone. It's time to shape up by seeking and using the right tools even if it means retraining or re-educating yourself. It's time to turn things around by knocking on the right doors even if it means risking rejection. It's time to ask, seek, knock, and believe that you will receive, find, and have access respectively.

> *It is time to ASK and believe that you will receive, find, and have access to all that you need.*

The change you seek will be initiated mostly in the form of a change in attitude or mindset, a discipline or an action step. The woman with the issue of blood *kept saying* to herself, "If only I can have access to the Master, I will be successful." (Matthew 9:21, paraphrased).

*Reflection*

Out of the seven roadblocks listed above, which three can you relate to the most?

What change in attitude, discipline or action step are you going to adopt to turn your giftedness to greatness?

*Confession*

Feel free to make up and write down your confession.

*Write down the relevant practical steps you need to make the new insight a reality, and the time to implement it.*

| Practical steps | Time |
|---|---|
| | |

# LEADERSHIP ACCELERATORS

*Scripture Reading*

*The Lord said to Samuel, How long will you mourn for Saul, seeing I have rejected him from reigning over Israel? Fill your horn with oil; I will send you to Jesse the Bethlehemite. For I have provided for Myself a king among his sons* (1 Samuel 16:1).

*The fastest way to develop your influence is to be a solution provider.*

*– Lakers Komaiya*

One of the chief indicators of the health of an economy is the unemployment rate. While this figure is understandably low for countries that are prospering, nations that are economically challenged are often plagued with many unemployed individuals. With high rates of unemployment, many people scramble for limited vacant positions. On occasions,

> *Potential leaders stimulate a total paradigm shift in their field of endeavour.*

a job advertisement for a single position attracts as many

as five hundred applicants. Although leadership positions may also be typically advertised, there are other numerous leadership spots that are "snatched" by individuals who understand the concept of leadership accelerators.

The following are leadership accelerators:

1. **Service**: When you are willing to serve and provide value to others, you are definitely on your way to increasing your influence with people. John C. Maxwell, famously quotes, "Leadership is influence."

2. **Unflinching dedication to a cause bigger than the individual**: Individuals who are personally committed to initiatives bigger than them are poised to attract and influence others with similar values.

3. **Participation in the BIG question**: What question or riddle are you drawn to solve? Mike Murdoch once remarked, "The problem that infuriates you the most is the one you have been assigned to solve."

4. **Provision of the BIG answer or solution**: The problem you are willing to solve determines who pursues and follows you. This is so because as you provide solutions to others, more people are drawn to you. Hence, you are placed in an enviable position of empowering people. In the process, you make them better, stronger, and greater.

5. **Strategically withstanding and overcoming adversity**: Abraham Lincoln said, "Nearly all men can stand adversity." However, only leaders use adversity as a stepping-stone to greatness. These individuals not only endure difficulties, they become better versions of themselves.

6. **Challenging old thinking and proffering new perspectives**: Potential leaders are willing to confront old assertions, behaviors, and standard operating procedures. They are often disrupters who provoke a new way of thinking or looking at things. They stimulate a total paradigm shift in their fields of endeavor.

7. **Influence with other strategic leaders**: If the function of leadership is to produce more leaders and not followers, as remarked by Ralph Nader, then individuals who strategically position themselves around leaders will be influenced by those leaders.

   Relationships with leaders around you will give you knowledge of how they think, behave, visualize, handle adversity and opportunity, collaborate, care, value, develop people, etc. Make it a duty to network with leaders in your field of influence or the area in which you are developing your greatness.

8. **Having a sense of calling, urgency, and being chosen to carry out a mission**: While followers are content with procrastinating, prospective leaders move swiftly and wisely to address matters arising. They have a sense that someone will "badly" depend on their A-game; therefore, they "bring it on!"

9. **Bringing hope for a present or future reality**: Individuals who are futurists nurture hope for the present and create a glorious expectation for the future. Do this, and you are sure to be a person who influences others.

*Reflection*
Leadership is about challenging old or out-of-date thinking and offering a fresh viewpoint. Have you been contemplating assertions in your field that may need revising?

What will happen if you turn upside-down or inside-out some of the claims or uncontested affirmations in your industry?

*Confession*
Feel free to make up and write down your confession.

*Write down the relevant practical steps you need to make the new insight a reality, and the time to implement it.*

| Practical steps | Time |
|---|---|
| | |

# A KING AMONG SONS

*Scripture Reading*

*The Lord said to Samuel, How long will you mourn for Saul, seeing I have rejected him from reigning over Israel? Fill your horn with oil; I will send you to Jesse the Bethlehemite. For I have provided for Myself a king among his sons* (1 Samuel 16:1).

*Times of transitions are strenuous, but I love them. They are an opportunity to purge, rethink priorities, and be intentional about new habits. We can make our new normal any way we want.*

*– Kristin Armstrong*

One of the constants in life is that seasons will always change. While some kingdoms face imminent demise, others continue to prosper, expand, and become more established. People come to the end of their assignments and others

> To the one who is not paying attention and clueless, everyone appears to be on the same level.

are prepared to take their places. Some are stuck in recurring life experiences; others graduate and are ready to be promoted to the next level. To the one who is not paying attention and clueless, everyone appears to be on the same level. But suddenly, some individuals are distinguished and elevated to the status of kings among sons.

What characteristics did David have? What competencies did he develop? What mindset did he cultivate? What behavior did he demonstrate? To what sacrifice did he commit to making him stand out and chosen to become king?

It appears God, as the ultimate leader and mentor, is always searching to delegate His authority to man. He is willing to empower individuals in a bid to demonstrate His power and might. The Lord's eyes keep on roaming throughout the earth, looking for those whose hearts completely belong to him, so that he may strongly support them (2 Chronicles 16:9, International Standard Version). He is always working in the background, preparing the next king to extend His dominion on earth. "Thy kingdom come. Thy will be done. As it is in heaven" (Matthew 6:10). When you, as one developing the greatness within, align yourself with God, you become an extension of all that He is. Always remember, "Greater is He that is in you than he that is in the world" (1 John 4:4).

What made David become distinguished among sons even though he had brothers who were older, more experienced, suited, skilled for certain assignments?

There are certain qualities you can exhibit that will make you prominent in the crowd.

These are:

1. Courage
2. Sacrifice
3. Commitment
4. Ability to generate influence
5. Teachability
6. Resilience
7. Passion and compassion

*Reflection*
Which top two qualities do you want to begin to work on from today?

*Confession*
Feel free to make up and write down your confession.

*Write down the relevant practical steps you need to make the new insight a reality, and the time to implement it.*

| Practical steps | Time |
|---|---|
| | |
| | |
| | |
| | |

# BE READY TO GO "ALL ABOUT"

*Scripture Reading*

*So the report of Him spread throughout all Syria, and they brought Him all who were sick, those afflicted with various diseases and torments, those under the power of demons, and epileptics, and paralysed people, and He healed them*
(Matthew 4:24).

*The aim of marketing is to know and understand the customer so well the product or service fits him and sells itself.*

*– Peter Drucker*

Greatness comes in different shapes and sizes. However, one thing that is common to them all is that intentional leaders have to be willing to go all about to spread their influence. They are relentless in making their offerings known to those in their world. The tools they use include the social

> *They are relentless in making their offerings known to those in their world.*

media, speaking to people one-on-one, giving presentations at seminars and conferences, and providing their services or products for free, at least, initially!

Jesus Christ modeled this to the present-day entrepreneur or "sociopreneur" by:

1. **Teaching**: He provided instructions – teaching people a new way of thinking, feeling, and behaving.
2. **Preaching**: He motivated and inspired people to become their best selves.
3. **Healing**: He offered solutions to problems. He never stopped at challenging old thoughts and perspectives. He showed people a new way to problem-solve.

Because Jesus was ready to qualify his clients (those who would benefit the most) and take His service to where they were, His enterprise became successful. The Scripture says, "So the report of Him spread throughout all Syria, and they brought Him all who were sick." If you want to enjoy such phenomenal growth in your endeavor, you have to be willing to meet the demands that may be placed on you and not complain about having too many clients or customers to serve.

*Reflection*

What are the 2 top quality services or products you offer people in your industry?

How reliable are your products and services in solving the challenges of clients?

*Confession*

Feel free to make up and write down your confession.

*Write down the relevant practical steps you need to make the new insight a reality, and the time to implement it.*

| Practical steps | Time |
| --- | --- |
|  |  |

# OPINION POLLS AND SERVICE

*Scripture Reading*

*Then [he] said to Jesse, Are all your sons here? [Jesse] said, There is yet the youngest; he is tending the sheep. Samuel said to Jesse, Send for him, for we will not sit down to eat until he is here* (1 Samuel 16:11).

*Don't let someone else's opinion of you become your reality.*

*– Les Brown*

Forgotten by his father, despised by an "indomitable" enemy soldier named Goliath, rejected by his siblings, and abhorred by the leader of his country — King Saul, David did not give much thought to people's estimation of him. This is an era in which the number of Facebook, Twitter, and Instagram likes are the predominant measures people use to evaluate how popular or accepted their views are. This, however, becomes unhealthy when our identities as leaders solely hinge on the acceptance or lack thereof on social media.

Below are a couple of lessons we can learn from David who later became one of the greatest kings in Israel:

1.  Leaders have healthy opinions of themselves. They are aware of what they possess and cherish their value. Even though others may want to sell them short, they do not live by people's opinions.

2.  Intentional leaders do not allow themselves to be related to as underdogs. They have a top-dog mentality, which is more concerned with adding value to others and being solution providers.

3.  Great leaders are not afraid to chart new or unexplored courses. Though the youngest in his family and at the time ineligible to enlist in the army, David remained visible to King Saul while he maintained loyalty to his father serving him.

4.  Leaders are willing to serve others even though they may not be called to the podium to get immediate recognition for their efforts. David knew he had something to offer. Nevertheless, he waited for the right timing. He understood the law of timing made popular by John C. Maxwell that states, "When to lead is as important as what to do and

> *When to lead is as important as what to do and where to go.*

where to go." He further commented, "The wrong action at the wrong time leads to disaster. The right action at the wrong time brings resistance. The wrong action at the right time is a mistake." However, "The right action at the right time results in success." Aspiring leaders understand that the gift of a man makes room for him and brings him before people of influence.

5. Intentional leaders are prepared such that when they are called, they are ready and able to deliver. How primed are you if provided the golden opportunity? What do you have to offer? What problem are you able to solve? There was a problem tailor-made for David to address. He promptly seized the opportunity when the occasion arose.

6. Leaders commit to the skillful exercise of their craft before deployment. David was already a skilled lyre player before he was called to minister to the Head of State. How are you currently handling what has been committed to you? Do you deliver your value excellently or do you simply do a shoddy job? Remember, time and chance happen to them all (Ecclesiastes 9:11). Your time is now. The problem waits. Are you ready to provide the solution?

*Reflection*

How do people's opinion of you shape your service delivery?

Are you always ready to bring on your A-game for those who really rely on it?

*Confession*

Feel free to make up and write down your confession.

*Write down the relevant practical steps you need to make the new insight a reality, and the time to implement it.*

| Practical steps | Time |
|---|---|
|  |  |

# GOD'S GROWTH PLAN

*Scripture Reading*

*I assure you, most solemnly I tell you, Unless a grain of wheat falls into the earth and dies, it remains [just one grain; it never becomes more but lives] by itself alone. But if it dies, it produces many others and yields a rich harvest (John 12:24).*

*Growth is painful. Change is painful. But, nothing is as painful as staying stuck where you do not belong.*
*— N. R. Narayana Murthy*

At times, the only thing you have is a "seed." When your possessions are limited, it is typical to be frugal as you want to keep what you have. To you, addition might be a most natural way to conceive increase. Therefore, the concept of losing to gain is oxymoronic. We gain to keep, so why should we lose again what we have got? Letting go means "sacrifice." Sacrifice indicates that you have to relinquish something precious to you. The

> *Sacrifice indicates that you have to relinquish something precious to you.*

interesting thing, however, is that no matter how lovely a seed is it remains only a grain unless it falls into the earth and dies. Death, in this respect, brings life. In other words, adversity can produce growth.

Looking at our scripture in the context of an emerging entrepreneur or a developing leader:

1. **A grain...remains alone**

   This suggests, "If you want to go fast, move alone. If you want to go far, move with others."

2. **Falls to the earth**

   No one wants to "fall." Falling is tough. We do not want to "fall" into collaboration. Teamwork may require us to be more accommodating of others than being "lone rangers." We typically prefer to remain perched in our comfort zones than risk the effort of forging a partnership with others to realize our objectives.

3. **Dies**

   This indicates we have to give up our comfort zones to reasonably do whatever it takes to bring our dreams to reality.

4. **Produces many others**

   This is the beginning of fruitfulness. When this happens, we begin to walk in the reality of the blessing: "Be fruitful and multiply and fill the earth and subdue it, and have dominion." (Genesis 1:28).

5. **Yields a harvest.**
   Your harvest yields more fruits, which bear more seeds, which are then planted to yield more harvest. The cycle is repeated.

A grain can choose to remain in the comfort of being nourished by a mother tree or decide to sacrifice her comfort by falling, dying to self, and allowing a normal process of reproduction to take place. A seed has the potential to become a forest. This, however, can only happen if the seed releases its potential by letting go and allowing itself to undergo the course of dying, which is a painful process.

*Reflection*
Which top two qualities do you want to begin to work on from today?

*Confession*
Feel free to make up and write down your confession.

*Write down the relevant practical steps you need to make the new insight a reality, and the time to implement it.*

| Practical steps | Time |
|---|---|
|  |  |

# HELP ME SOLVE THIS PROBLEM

*Scripture Reading*

*Martha replied, I know that he will rise again in the resurrection at the last day* (John 11:24).

*A successful person isn't necessarily better than her less successful peers at solving problems; her pattern-recognition facilities have just learned what problems are worth solving.*

*– Ray Kurzweil*

As you work towards developing the greatness within, you will be provided with opportunities to be a solution provider. The context may be at home, work, within your team or even on the playground. People typically look up to individuals who can offer direction and provide answers to problems. While some challenges are easily solved, others may require cracking a code. Martha sought the key to a

> *People typically look up to individuals who can offer direction and provide answers to problems.*

problem that seemed to defy a solution. When you find yourself in Martha's shoes, consider the following:

1. What questions are you asking? Leaders ask the right questions that point them to the right answers. Because they are more interested in asking the right questions than attempting to give an answer from a limited perspective, they get directions to the right solution.

2. What framework or paradigm are you using to understand the scope of your problem? Leaders are not particularly limited by a lone framework. They are open to various prospects and possibilities.

3. What collaborations are you seeking? Leaders are willing to seek the necessary support and associate with others who are in positions to facilitate a solution to their questions.

4. What crucial element of the proposition are you missing? We cannot possibly have a 360-degree view of all that is around us. Leaders are willing to have others point out to them what may be in their blind spots.

5. What self-limiting beliefs may be undermining your ability to find a solution? As most people are blinded by old ideas and viewpoints, they have an expectation of a solution that is simply in front of them, waiting to be acknowledged. Leaders, however, recognize and rise above existing philosophies and knowledge that may restrain them from accessing a solution.

6. I agree that leaders can benefit from hindsight and foresight. However, don't be too future-focused and miss out on the blessing that may be staring you down in the present. At times, we look for complicated answers to our challenges because we struggle to accept the simple ones that have been offered in the moment.

7. Finally, ensure that your thoughts and words are congruous with your actions. Martha could say the right things; yet, she struggled to believe the right things. There seemed to be a disconnect between her words, beliefs, and behavior.

*Reflection*

Of the seven points addressed above, in which area do you struggle the most when you are brainstorming or problem-solving?

How do you intend to address this?

*Confession*

Feel free to make up and write down your confession.

*Write down the relevant practical steps you need to make the new insight a reality, and the time to implement it.*

| Practical steps | Time |
| --- | --- |
| | |

# LESSON 47

# WHEN TO BREAK THE "IN CASE OF EMERGENCY" GLASS

*Scripture Reading*
*Therefore [even] when He heard that Lazarus was sick,*
*He still stayed two days longer in the same place where*
*He was* (John 11:6).

*Panic causes tunnel vision. Calm acceptance of danger*
*allows us to more easily assess the situation and see the*
*option*

*– Simon Sinek*

We all maintain a sense of cool when things are going pretty well. The kids are doing well in school; you have money stashed in your savings account; the return on your investment portfolio is brilliant; business and ministry are experiencing explosive growth. You believe you have finally secured great relationships and affiliations that will protect you from any surprises. But then, without warning, adversity strikes!

You are at the brink of bankruptcy, facing a foreclosure or repossession. You are falling behind on your mortgage repayments and your creditors are all over you. Your family has bailed out on you and friends have deserted you. You are lonely, crushed, and perplexed. How do you respond in panic situations? How are some people able to "keep it together" when everyone around them is losing their shirts?

Mary and Martha had a reason to panic. They had suffered the loss of their beloved brother. Like most individuals, they saw the need to transfer their anxiety, fear, and grief unto someone else. This, indeed, is a serious issue. Hence, an SOS was sent to Jesus. They expected Him to drop everything and race to the scene of the chaos. Jesus, however, took a different approach. He practiced the law of timing: "When to lead is as important as what to do and where to go" (John C. Maxwell).

> *One of the marks of a great leader is stillness in the eye of the storm.*

In contrast to followers that may be flustered by unexpected events, one of the marks of a great leader is stillness in the eye of the storm. This was not the only time Jesus demonstrated composure in panic situations. He was calm:

- **In the face of lack**
  On two occasions when wine ran out at a banquet (John 2:3) and when He needed to feed 5,000 people in the wilderness (Matthew 14:13-21).
- **In the face of loss**
  He raised Lazarus from the dead (John 11:38-44).

- **In the face of ill fortune**
  He spoke peace to the raging storm (Mark 4:35-41).
- **In the face of satanic attacks**
  He overcame Satan by the revealed Word of God (Matthew 4:4).
- **In the face of betrayal**
  He fixed the right ear of Malchus, the high priest's servant, which one of the disciples cut off shortly before Jesus was arrested (Luke 22:50-51).
- **In the face of sin and death**
  Though without sin, Jesus gave up his life that people who believe in Him might have life in abundance (John 10:10).

Your capacity to remain peaceful in the face of adversity will determine your effectiveness as an emerging leader.

*Reflection*
What situations typically cause you to panic?
What do you need to know, learn, and practice to maintain calm in challenging times?

*Confession*
Feel free to make up and write down your confession.

*Write down the relevant practical steps you need to make the new insight a reality, and the time to implement it.*

| Practical steps | Time |
|---|---|
|  |  |
|  |  |
|  |  |
|  |  |

# CHOOSE YOUR BATTLES

*Scripture Reading*
*So from that day on they took counsel and plotted how they might put Him to death* (John 11:53).

*Everybody certainly has the right to defend themselves. That's not to say that they should defy common sense by avoiding or diffusing confrontation.*

*– Steven Seagal*

Jesus has pulled off one of the greatest miracles in history — bringing back to life someone who had been dead four days. In our times, this would have gone viral on different platforms on social media with hashtag, "This is unreal." Aside from the fact that this was an astonishing feat, Jesus brought back to life a dear friend thereby putting an end to a burgeoning grief.

But wait! I thought the world should rejoice that he who was dead is now alive. Ideally, yes. However, in reality, although you may be fulfilling your mission, bringing value to people and influencing your community, some people will be unhappy about your success.

At times, success in one area might threaten or de-stabilize existing establishments. It is at this point that your exploits may begin to attract a backlash. But wait! How do you personally handle other people's successes too? How have you trained your team members to respond to the achievements of other organizations?

During Jesus Christ's earthly ministry, the leaders of the religious organizations had sidekicks that did recon and reported activities that may undermine their established institutions. I can't imagine how Jesus Christ would have felt having a ransom hanging over His head simply because He had just experienced a huge career success. Did He feel the urge to counterattack and deal a decisive blow to His challengers?

Earlier, when Jesus was addressing His team, He affirmed that His Father, His Mentor, hears and listens to Him always. This indicates that godly wisdom is required to decipher when to stand your ground and when to back off. Here, Jesus said not a word to the Pharisees but simply withdrew to be with His disciples. Be smart enough to choose your battles. There is a time to stand up and fight but there is also a time to retreat, strategize, and consolidate your mission.

> *Wisdom is required to decipher when to stand your ground and when to back off.*

*Reflection*

How do you respond to what you may perceive as a personal attack or criticism of your leadership style?

How do you respond to people's opinions of your achievement and success?

How could you have prevented yourself from getting involved in unnecessary battles in the past?

How different would you act in the future?

*Confession*
Feel free to make up and write down your confession.

*Write down the relevant practical steps you need to make the new insight a reality, and the time to implement it.*

| Practical steps | Time |
|---|---|
| | |

# DO NOT BE AN "UNDERMINER "

*Scripture Reading*

*For rebellion is as the sin of witchcraft, and stubbornness is as idolatry and teraphim [household good luck images]. Because you have rejected the word of the Lord, He also has rejected you being from being king* (I Samuel 15:23).

*Obedience is an act of faith; disobedience is the result of unbelief.*

*– Edwin Louis Cole*

A clear instruction was given to this leader when he was charged with carrying out a specific duty. He assembled his team; they geared themselves appropriately and proceeded to carry out the assignment. Clinically executed, the campaign was a huge success. Then this leader tripped. He listened to the people's voice. Their demand was in sharp contrast to the instruction he was given before the campaign. In his mind, he would have thought, "The customer is always right." In this case, the people were his customers and he wanted to satisfy their demands. This meant he was not going to be compliant with his leader's directive.

Intentionally disobeying God's directive is viewed as mutiny. In other words, it is regarded as staging a coup with a view to dethrone God as the lead individual in your life — rejecting His leadership and installing yourself as the new commander. Notice that God, however, did not reject Saul as a person. He only vetoed him from being "king." That is because insubordination, which equates to stubbornness, is regarded as being obstinately set in one's way and purpose.

When you flagrantly disobey your superior, you demonstrate to your team members that he/she is not worth listening to. Undermining your boss shows you up as someone who lacks integrity. Do not allow your personal struggle with self-esteem and the need for self-promotion make you succumb to "the wish of the people." When you feel provoked to go against your leader's command, consider the following:

> *Undermining your boss shows you up as someone who lacks integrity.*

1. Check your motive
2. Bear in mind the repercussions of your behavior
3. Seek clarification with your leader
4. Understand that, to lead, you have to learn to submit and be willing to be led by a superior entity. Disobedience disqualifies you from leadership.

5. Recognize who has the power and who has the authority.

The disobedience that leads to rejection or dismissal does not happen in a day. It is a culmination of several acts of waywardness that were left unchecked.

*Reflection*
In which area of your personal or professional life have you been guilty of disobedience?

What steps can you take to address the issue that may be causing you to be disobedient, especially to people or organizations that may be overseeing you?

*Confession*
Feel free to make up and write down your confession.

*Write down the relevant practical steps you need to make the new insight a reality, and the time to implement it.*

| Practical steps | Time |
|---|---|
|  |  |
|  |  |
|  |  |
|  |  |

# LESSON 50
# THREAT-ALERT

*Scripture Reading*
*I went out after it and smote it and delivered the lamb out of its mouth; and when it arose against me, I caught it by its beard and smote it and killed it* (1 Samuel 17:35).

*Courage – a perfect sensibility of the measure of danger, and a mental willingness to endure it.*
                    *– William Tecumseh Sherman*

Leaders do not take chances against threats that may undermine what has been committed to their care. They understand that giving in to such terrors will set up a pattern of behavior that may ultimately destroy what has been entrusted to their care.

1.  Be cognizant of perceived threats that may be lodged in your mind. Even though unreal, they remain potent and dangerous with the ability to emasculate your personal or organizational plans and objectives. These threats include fear, anxiety, doubt, indecision, discouragement etc.

2. Be careful of subtle threats that operate "under the radar" in your life. These include unhelpful thoughts, maladaptive habits that have become "part" of you, things that have been compartmentalized in your mind as "impossible," secret pleasures that may drain instead of revitalize your energy and momentum etc.

3. Be aware and take steps to address real threats that may put the realization of your goals, objectives, and vision in jeopardy. These risks are audacious and set to wipe you and your vision out. They mince no words in letting you know that their mission is to undermine everything you stand for.

Leaders develop the habit and organizational culture that take on challenges, which may undermine the life of the service or product they offer. This they do by helping themselves and others to:

1. Assess for and identify threats or risks
2. Be clear about the impact of the threat if left unattended
3. Design a strategy to address the risk
4. Neutralize the threat
5. Be cognizant and continue to monitor the health of self, system, and the organization in general
6. Guard against future threats

You have an active part to play in challenging and bringing under control personal and organizational threats and attacks. Learn to leverage your skills, competencies, determination, courage, and contribution from team members where necessary. However, you don't have to fight your threats or address your risks alone. There is an unseen force that is behind you as you make the move to neutralize the menaces. Remember, you can do all things through Christ who gives you strength (Philippians 4:13).

> *You don't have to fight your threats or address your risks alone.*

## Reflection

What threats have you identified that may be undermining your life, service, product or organization?

How do you intend to neutralize these threats?

## Confession

Feel free to make up and write down your confession.

*Write down the relevant practical steps you need to make the new insight a reality, and the time to implement it.*

| Practical steps | Time |
|-----------------|------|
|  |  |

# Conclusion

I hope you are super-motivated to deploy the fresh insights you have gleaned to develop the greatness within. It has been a pleasure sharing these lessons with you. If you commit to and deploy the practical steps you have noted after each lesson, you cannot but begin to unleash the greatness within you.

The whole world awaits your manifestation.

# DOWNLOAD FREE RESOURCES

Just to say thank you for buying my book, I would like to give you the "Developing the Greatness Within You" assessment FREE!

## TO DOWNLOAD, GO TO:

http:www.tribeofdavid.com.au/resources

Made in the USA
Las Vegas, NV
16 June 2022